# THE WAR TO OUST SADDAM HUSSEIN

# THE WAR TO OUST SADDAM HUSSEIN

*Just War and the New Face of Conflict*

JAMES TURNER JOHNSON

ROWMAN & LITTLEFIELD PUBLISHERS, INC.
*Lanham • Boulder • New York • Toronto • Oxford*

ROWMAN & LITTLEFIELD PUBLISHERS, INC.

Published in the United States of America
by Rowman & Littlefield Publishers, Inc.
A wholly owned subsidiary of The Rowman & Littlefield Publishing Group, Inc.
4501 Forbes Boulevard, Suite 200, Lanham, Maryland 20706
www.rowmanlittlefield.com

PO Box 317 Oxford, OX2 9RU, UK

Distributed by National Book Network

British Library Cataloguing in Publication Information Available

**Library of Congress Cataloging-in-Publication Data**

Johnson, James Turner.
   The war to oust Saddam Hussein : just war and the new face of conflict / James
Turner Johnson.
      p.   cm.
   Includes bibliographical references and index.
   ISBN 0-7425-4956-9 (cloth : alk. paper)
   1. Iraq War, 2003—Moral and ethical aspects.   2. Just war doctrine.   3. Hussein,
Saddam, 1937–   I. Title.
   DS79.76.J64 2005
   956.7044'3—dc22                                                          2005009319

Printed in the United States of America

∞ ™ The paper used in this publication meets the minimum requirements of American
National Standard for Information Sciences—Permanence of Paper for Printed Library
Materials, ANSI/NISO Z39.48-1992.

# CONTENTS

ACKNOWLEDGMENTS                                          vii

PART I    SETTING THE CONTEXT: ARE WE
          INVOLVED IN A CLASH OF
          CIVILIZATIONS?

1    JIHAD AND JUST WAR: ETHICAL PERSPECTIVES
     ON THE NEW FACE OF CONFLICT                          3

2    DISCIPLINING JUST WAR THINKING: USES AND
     MISUSES OF THE JUST WAR IDEA IN RECENT
     AMERICAN DEBATE                                     23

PART II   THE WAR TO OUST SADDAM HUSSEIN:
          BEFORE

3    THE DEBATE OVER USING FORCE AGAINST THE
     SADDAM HUSSEIN REGIME: WAS THE USE OF
     FORCE JUSTIFIED?                                    45

PART III  THE WAR TO OUST SADDAM HUSSEIN:
          DURING

4    OPERATION IRAQI FREEDOM: A MORALIST'S
     NOTEBOOK                                            71

PART IV   THE WAR TO OUST SADDAM HUSSEIN:
AFTER

5   LOOKING BACK AS A WAY OF LOOKING AHEAD   113

BIBLIOGRAPHY   147

INDEX   151

ABOUT THE AUTHOR   159

# ACKNOWLEDGMENTS

While the majority of this book was written during 2003 and 2004 and the final work on it was done in late 2004, the first three chapters reflect a number of papers and other presentations I gave during the period immediately following the attacks of September 11, 2001, through the spring of 2004. I am grateful to the following institutions for the invitations that led to these presentations and the discussions that followed (listed in chronological order): the Norwegian Military Academy; the Pew Forum; the University of Michigan Law School; the Center for Public Justice; the Professional Military Ethics Center of the U.S. Naval Academy; the Carnegie Center for Ethics and International Affairs; the Carr Center of Harvard University; Howard Paine University, Brownwood, Texas; Brown University; Hanover College, Hanover, Indiana; the U.S. Naval War College; the Center for the Study of Religion and the Woodrow Wilson School of Princeton University; the Foreign Policy Research Institute of Philadelphia; Wheaton College; Salisbury University, Salisbury, Maryland; the Program on Humanitarian Policy and Conflict Research, Harvard Law School; the George C. Marshall Center, Garmisch-Partenkirchen, Germany; the Chautauqua Lecture Program of Eastern Kentucky University, Richmond, Kentucky; Roanoke College, Roanoke, Virginia; the Center for the Study of World Religions of Doshisha University, Kyoto, Japan; and the Gregorian University, Rome, Italy.

# I

# SETTING THE CONTEXT: ARE WE INVOLVED IN A CLASH OF CIVILIZATIONS?

# 1

# JIHAD AND JUST WAR

## Ethical Perspectives on the
## New Face of Conflict

### ARE WE INVOLVED IN A "CLASH OF CIVILIZATIONS"?

The attacks on America of September 11, 2001, forced Americans to confront the contemporary phenomenon of terrorism as never before and also to face with some urgency an uncomfortable question: Is America, and more broadly Western culture as a whole, involved in a clash of civilizations with the world of Islam? This question, famously posed by Samuel P. Huntington in his widely discussed article "The Clash of Civilizations?" in 1993, effectively challenged the assumptions of political realism, which discounted the importance of civilizational or cultural influences on political behavior, including the use of armed force, by predicting that the most important future conflicts are likely to arise along the "cultural fault lines" separating major civilizations. "Differences among civilizations are not only real; they are basic," Huntington argued, noting that these differences include "history, language, culture, tradition, and, most important, religion" (25). In sum, he wrote,

> These differences are the product of centuries. They will not soon disappear. They are far more fundamental than differences among political ideologies and political regimes. Differences do not necessarily mean conflict, and conflict does not necessarily mean violence. Over the centuries, however, differences among civilizations have generated the most prolonged and the most violent conflicts. (25)

Although little noticed at the time, Huntington's argument echoed that of an earlier scholar, Quincy Wright, whose *A Study of War*, first published in the

1940s, was the first major effort to examine war, its causes, and the possibilities of its limitation from the perspective of modern social science. Wright observed that every culture has generated its own "body of doctrine reconciling the religious, ethical, and economic values of the civilization and the political and legal values of the particular state with the practices of war" (155). Those understandings and the rules for war coming out of them break down at the boundaries distinguishing one culture from another; as a result, Wright observed (as Huntington did later), wars across such boundaries have historically been more violent and less subject to restraint. The potential for conflict across those boundaries is, at the same time, aggravated by the fact that every culture makes universal claims about matters of deep importance to itself: where these differ from the claims made by another culture, this difference may cause or inflame conflict.

One respondent to Huntington who did note the thematic connections between him and earlier scholars, including Wright, was Albert L. Weeks, who observed that Huntington's article had resurrected "an old controversy in the study of international affairs" (24): that between partisans of the nation-state as the basic unit of world politics and those who "view world affairs on the lofty level of the civilizations to which nation-states belong" (24–25). Weeks went on to discount the latter approach, arguing that the "cultural and religious glue" that allegedly holds civilizations together is "thin and cracked," in contrast to the much more powerful forces associated with the nation-state. Fouad Ajami argued similarly that "civilizations do not control states, states control civilizations." He found it comparatively easy to support this judgment by reference to the Gulf War of 1990–1991: "The fight in the gulf was seen for what it was: a bid for primacy [by Saddam Hussein's Iraq] met by an imperial expedition [which included forces from Muslim states] that laid it to waste" (9).

And so on. Although the idea of a "clash of civilizations" was hotly debated for a while, this was a debate among members of an academic and foreign affairs elite, and few outside that elite took notice of or even knew about the debate. Moreover, in the circles of practical politics, how to deal with states posed the immediate problem, while how to deal with civilizations seemed vague and abstract. Academic training for service in policy positions continued to stress the identification and analysis of concrete political and economic interests as the basis for state action, not cultural or civilizational factors. The influence of religion in particular on political action was hard to accept: as a 1994 book title put it (aiming to try to change the situation), religion was *The Missing Dimension of Statecraft*.

Why should such a debate, however hot for a time, matter for thinking about public policy in general and war in particular? Why should it matter whether policy and decision makers consider religion in their practice of statecraft? The answer lies in the assumptions they bring to their roles. When civilizational factors are bracketed out of consideration, as happened with religion in thinking about and practicing politics according to the model of political realism, or are minimized relative to concerns deemed more concrete, immediate, and pressing—"interests," in the term of realist analysis—and when it turns out that these factors are indeed central to the motivations behind the actions of people intent upon harming us and able to do so in unpredicted and disastrous ways, and when those people are not in fact organized into a state with its own "interests," then assumptions that allow no room for this are clearly inadequate. The September 11 attacks and the subsequent global war on terrorism have required coming face to face with the possibility that this conflict is indeed, in a vary basic way, a clash of civilizations. In this context, the important questions have to do with the extent to which there is such a fundamental clash and the extent to which there is not, questions that cannot be answered with a simple affirmation or denial or put on hold by referring the "clash of civilizations" idea to a decades-old debate among academic elites.

But old assumptions die hard. Not only is it much more complicated and difficult to think about civilizations and cultures rather than states and interests, but one of the most deeply embedded legacies of the Enlightenment in Western thought is that religion and politics have their own spheres and should not be mixed. This conception was historically not simply the fruit of rational reflection but was a reaction to the horrors of the post-Reformation religious wars in Europe; the separation of religion from politics was an attempt to prevent such carnage from happening again. The nature and degree of this separation is, of course, understood and institutionalized differently in different Western societies, but the fundamental conception of such separation is deeply embedded in Western notions of politics as an essentially secular activity. Al Qaeda's appeal to a radical form of Islam appears, from this perspective, as deeply alien and deeply wrong. But—and this is where the idea of a clash of civilizations begins to appear—this appeal is not equally alien to ways of thinking in Islamic history and tradition, where a link between religion and politics is assumed to characterize the good society. If religion should have nothing to do with political life—the Enlightenment legacy—then how do we distinguish the terrorists from Islamic culture as a whole?

The attempt to make such a distinction led to a variety of tactics in the commentary on the September 11 attacks. In the immediate aftermath, President George W. Bush attempted to mark off the religious justification claimed by al Qaeda from Islamic religion proper, calling Islam a "religion of peace." Subsequently, several evangelical Christians took the opposite tack, pulling al Qaeda's terrorism together with Islam as a whole by arguing that Islam is a religion of the sword in which God mandates fighting against unbelievers. Two prominent writers for the *New York Times* took their own lines. Shortly after the September 11 attacks, Judith Miller, author of *God Has Ninety-Nine Names*, a book on Middle Eastern political figures and movements, made the rounds of the talk shows arguing the thesis she had advanced in that book, that the terrorists were using religion as an ideological cover for their own political goals so that the attacks were not in fact grounded in religion at all. A few weeks later, in the Sunday *New York Times Magazine*, the second writer, Andrew Sullivan, published an article on the war against terrorism in which he took an opposite tack, assimilating the attacks to religious fundamentalism as a more general phenomenon and arguing that if fundamentalism were eradicated, then terrorism—or at least terrorism in the name of religion—would disappear. Both of these approaches express ways of denying that "real" religion has anything to do with terrorism. But both, it seems to me, miss the point; the truth lies somewhere in between.

We should make no mistake that al Qaeda's justification for its actions is a specifically religious appeal. Religion and politics are tied together in the rationale for terrorism against America and the West and the motivation of particular terrorists. Saying that appeals to religion are just a cover for political goals fails to come to terms with this basic fact. To do so assumes the division between religion and politics deriving from the Enlightenment but not shared within normative Islam. Further, this position overlooks the genuine religious fervor observably present in both the justifying appeals to Islamic tradition and in the motivation of individual terrorists. We may not like this use of religion—indeed, within Islam itself, knowledgeable, authoritative people have condemned it as wrongheaded—yet, it is genuinely religious, and we do not understand the link between Islam and terrorism properly if we do not recognize this, seek to understand it, and join its critics within the sphere of Islam in seeking to counter it.

As to fundamentalism, there is no doubt that the terrorist appeals to Islamic tradition are appeals to versions of that tradition that have been called "fundamentalist." But fundamentalism is a broad term that does not always have the same meaning from one religion to another, or even within a given religion. Different forms of fundamentalism are linked to inward religious revival, to ethical renewal, to sustained efforts to provide needed social services, and to other results that are clearly in support of peace and human well-being, not to terror and other forms of violence. So, the problem of terrorism is not fundamentalism itself but the particular use it makes of a particular form of belief.

Sorting this out is an important step toward understanding the terrorists, thus an important step towards protecting ourselves from them and ultimately eliminating their threat entirely. That implies coming to understand more about the values and traditions embedded in the religion and culture of Islam. Saying this returns us once more to Huntington, who in the concluding paragraph of his "The Clash of Civilizations?" offered his own prescription for avoiding or mitigating conflict across civilizational lines: the West must "develop a more profound understanding of the basic religious and philosophical assumptions underlying other civilizations and the ways in which people in those civilizations see their interests. [This] will require an effort to identify elements of commonality between Western and other civilizations" (49). Wright had made much the same argument. But if we are to make good sense of the values and traditions of the religion and culture of Islam, the war against terrorism also implies that we must understand more about the values and traditions of Western culture and the form of civilization it has produced.

The cultures of the West and of Islam have produced two distinct moral traditions concerning the right use of force, that of *just war* and that of the *jihad of the sword*. In the following pages, I examine each, identifying their main features, sketching their origins and development in their respective cultural contexts, noting how each conceives the relation of religion to political life, and comparing their content on three elements essential to both: the authority necessary for justified resort to armed force, the justifying causes, and right conduct in the use of justified force. I begin with the origin and development of the tradition of jihad of the sword in normative Islamic juristic thought. Then, I turn to the critical question of terrorism's appeal to the tradition of jihad: How far is this legitimate in the tradition's own terms and how far is it a distortion of that tradition? I examine this first with a specific look at al Qaeda's self-justifying language and, later, in the context of the use of terrorist methods by insurgents in the war in Iraq. My engagement with the just war tradition in this book is more extensive and more personal, for this is the moral tradition of the use of armed force that has come out of Western culture and that continues to express fundamental values in this culture. It is, I think, important to get the meaning of the just war idea right and to take it seriously in framing our actions, our views on the actions of others, and our thoughts about the sort of future we would like to achieve. With specific focus on the Iraq war, this is the subject of the rest of this book.

## THE TRADITION OF JIHAD OF THE SWORD

While the religion of Islam is ultimately based on the Qur'an, understood as divine revelation to the prophet Muhammad, its normative historical form has been that of a religion of law, a religion whose meaning is described by the interpretations provided by the recognized juristic schools. On the subject of the Islamic state, its relations with non-Islamic societies, and the idea of jihad as the form of war between the Islamic and non-Islamic worlds, the juristic tradition coalesced early in the era of the Abbasid caliphs, with the definitive work being done in the late eighth and early ninth centuries CE (second and third centuries AH). Central to this conception was a division of the world into two realms, that of the *dar al-islam*, or "territory of Islam," that is, the Islamic community, and the remainder of the world, defined as the *dar al-harb*, or "territory of war." (For fuller discussion of this distinction and the related ideas treated below, see my *Morality and Contemporary Warfare*, particularly chapters 3 and 4.)

The dar al-islam, as the jurists understood it, had existed since its creation by the prophet Muhammad himself, who was its first head. It is a community at the same time religious and political, and just as the Prophet himself had held both religious and political authority over the original community of Muslims, so the ruler of the dar al-islam, like the Prophet himself, was understood as having supremacy in both religion and politics. In theory, as the jurists developed this concept, there can be only one dar al-islam and only one right ruler, whom they understood to be the successor of the Prophet (the word "caliph"—*khalifa* in Arabic—can be translated as both "deputy" and "successor") and the inheritor of his authority in both the religious and political spheres. The classic jurists made no provision for a plurality of Muslim states or a plurality of Muslim rulers. Although the Sunni and Shia traditions differed on the criteria for selection of this ruler and on his title—caliph for the Sunnis, imam for the Shia—they both held to this fundamental theory of a single Muslim community and a single legitimate ruler. Because of its character—its unity, its rule by a successor of the Prophet, its governance according to divinely given law, the sharia—the dar al-islam as understood by the jurists is defined as fundamentally different from the rest of the world, which they saw as different in all these respects and, as a result, torn by perpetual conflict within itself, as well as the source of war directed toward the dar al-islam. A genuine, lasting, universal peace is possible, on the classical juristic conception, only when the dar al-harb is no more, when the whole world has become the dar al-islam, the space in which submission to God (*islam* in Arabic means "submission") is the law of the land. Until then, war between the two territories is the normal state of affairs, and the Islamic community must deal with it.

While treaties with one or another entity from the dar al-harb might preserve peace for a while, the only ultimate solution, as the early jurists conceived it, will be the complete triumph of the dar al-islam. In pursuit of this aim, the jurists developed the idea of jihad as the form of war waged on behalf of the dar al-islam against the dar al-harb. The fundamental meaning of the idea of jihad as found in the Qur'an is striving (in the path of God) by three means: the heart, the tongue, and the hand. In the Qur'an, the term *jihad* is never used for warfare; another word, *qital* (fighting), is used there. But the idea that striving in the path of God might require use of the sword is very early, and the jurists developed this idea, an extension of the jihad of the hand, to mean warfare on behalf of the dar al-islam. As they described it, this warfare could take either of two forms: the jihad of collective duty and that of individual duty. More fully, the former encompassed offensive jihad of the sword, occasioned by the general threat posed by the dar al-harb, waged by the dar al-islam as a collectivity under the authority of its legitimate ruler, the caliph for the Sunni tradition, the imam for the Shiites. The jihad of individual duty, by contrast, was limited to defense in the face of a dire emergency; such defensive jihad was described as occasioned by a direct attack upon the dar al-islam by a force from some part of the dar al-harb, when every Muslim was obligated to fight in defense on his own authority.

This classic formulation of the ideal Islamic community and its relation to the non-Islamic world remains in normative Islamic tradition. While it was never, even at the time of its formulation, an actual description of the religious and political arrangements within the world of Islam, it took powerful hold as an ideal for the Muslim community and as a basis for Muslim self-identification throughout the Islamic world. As a statement of fundamental Islamic values applied to the shaping of human community and the end toward which such community should aim, it continues to have power. Its direct analogue in Western thought is the city of God as described by St. Augustine. But just as with the city of God idea, there have been diverse ways of conceptualizing how to apply this goal to empirical human societies in history, or how to structure human societies so as to manifest respect for this end in the here and now. This conception of the dar al-islam, its relation to the remainder of the world, and the place of resort to the sword in service of that community does not directly and automatically translate to what contemporary radical Islamists, including terrorists, read into it.

For one thing, there is general agreement throughout Islam today that offensive jihad is no longer possible: for the Shia, it has not been possible since the occultation of the twelfth imam in the ninth century CE, for the Sunnis, since the end of the caliphate, dated either to the death of the last Abbasid caliph in the sixteenth century CE or to the end of the Ottoman state in 1924. The reason is that the requisite authority for such jihad no longer exists. One way of responding to this historical fact is to seek to reestablish the lost religiopolitical authority, either, for the Sunnis, by reestablishing the caliphate (said to be the goal of the Taliban leader Mullah Omar, with himself as chief candidate) or, for the Shia, by establishing an authoritative link to the imam who is in occultation (an idea behind the Iranian theocracy). Without such an authority to lead in a jihad of communal obligation, however, all that is left is the possibility of the jihad of individual duty, that is, the idea of jihad as defense against the aggression of the dar al-harb, the territory of war.

The model the jurists had in mind for defensive jihad was simple and quite circumscribed: a direct attack across the borders of the dar al-islam in a particular place, staged by the forces of whatever entity from the dar al-harb happened to be in that place. Against this attack, Muslims in the area were to rise up as a *levée en masse*. Whereas in offensive jihad only the best warriors were to form the army, in defensive jihad everyone, even women and children, had the personal obligation to try to stop the invader. While specific rules for fighting, especially for giving advance notice of hostilities and avoidance of harm to noncombatants, were specified for offensive jihad, these did not apply in the case of defensive jihad, where the enemy to be fought were the enemy's army, who were all combatants and who had already commenced hostilities by their aggression. So, the idea of defensive jihad, as originally developed, was quite restricted by context. The jurists did not make defensive jihad the normative case; they did not want to define an interpretation of Islamic law that would allow individual Muslims or self-constituted groups to take arms and institute an offense into the dar al-harb on their own, for that would be a threat to the unity and peace of the dar al-islam itself.

Such was the conception of jihad of the sword laid out normatively in the classic Islamic juristic tradition. Its fundamental form was that of the jihad of collective duty, striving in the path of God by the community of Islam as a body. It was, in its fundamentals, a conception in which the justified use of armed force was linked directly to the nature of that community, its historical purpose, and its preservation against the forces of disorder, which the jurists linked to absence of rule according to divine law. It was to be fought as an effort of that community as a whole, with some serving in the army and others serving the community in other ways. Authority and responsibility for such jihad lay with whoever was recognized as inheritor of the religious and political authority of the prophet Muhammad. Conduct in the normative idea of jihad of the sword was restricted by the words of the Prophet and by the example of the early (the "rightly guided") caliphs, who imposed rules for fighting similar in fundamental respects to the rules for just war that were later developed in Western cultural tradition. Only in cases of dire emergency, in the face of an invasion of the territory of the dar al-islam, the territory governed by God's law, thus the territory of peace, could individual Muslims take up the sword on their own authority, and when the emergency ended—when the invaders turned back, or when the army of the dar al-islam as a whole came onto the scene to take up the fight—that individual duty of the individual to fight once again gave way to the collective duty to support the jihad of the community as a whole.

The key was the matter of authority for jihad of the sword. In addition to the model laid down in the normative juristic tradition, two other ideas are found in Islamic history. One is a concept of authority for jihad warfare associated with the medieval warrior Saladin (Salah-al-din), who, although not the caliph and not directly acting on caliphal authority, led a Muslim army to victory over the forces of the crusaders in the Second Crusade. Saladin was a regional emir, or commander, and in terms of the juristic conception, his actions could be fitted within the frame of the jihad of individual duty: he and all his force fought, in the absence of a force from the caliph, out of their own individual duty to oppose the crusaders' taking of Muslim lands; he simply organized and directed their effort. The second historical idea is that of the *ghazi*, or leader in war, believed to have received a direct divine grace or blessing (*baraka*). This was an old idea, one that first appeared during the same period in which the classic juristic conception came together. Its most forceful form, though, came later, when the Turkish warlords and later the Sultans took the term as their own. The idea here was that divine authority to lead in jihad could be seen in its results: if the war was successful, that implied that the leader had received the divine blessing. Both these ideas fitted well within the concept of the jihad of emergency, that of individual duty.

With these and other ideas as their building material, the last hundred years or so have seen a development of the idea of defensive jihad that takes it well beyond its original context and increasingly distorts its meaning. First, at the end of the nineteenth century and in the early part of the twentieth, it became part of the ideology of the anticolonial struggle, whereby the presence of governments imposed by the colonial powers was defined as an aggression from the dar al-harb against the dar al-islam, so that any and all Muslims were justified in using armed force to throw out the colonial governments, as well as, perhaps, all of the elements of the colonial society or culture that had taken root under colonial hegemony. Local rulers and tribal leaders who led their followers in war in this struggle sometimes evoked the name of Saladin, and sometimes their authority derived from their success in war, interpreted by their followers as a sign that they possessed the divine baraka. By the 1970s and 1980s, the conception of colonialism as aggression against the dar al-islam requiring all Muslims to oppose it by force had developed to justify armed struggle in such predominantly Muslim states as Iran, Egypt, and Algeria against rulers who, while nominally Muslim, were deemed in fact to be apostates, governing as tools of the West according to non-Islamic purposes. Interesting in this development is the definition of the dar al-islam not as a unitary religiopolitical community with its special form of government but rather as any territory whose population is predominantly Muslim and that was at one time part of the formal religiopolitical community ruled by a designated successor to the prophet Muhammad. By this definition, any non-Islamic state established throughout the area once ruled by Islam must be resisted. Since the rules of restraint that apply in the jihad of collective duty do not apply in the case of emergency defensive jihad, the war against non-Islamic influences becomes one that in principle may be waged without restraint. The implications of this can be seen in the Palestinian armed struggle against Israel, which is religiously justified as defensive jihad. By definition, on these terms, the state of Israel is illegitimate since it stands on land that once was part of the dar al-islam and still properly belongs to it. All Israelis, and all of their supporters who happen to be in the state of Israel, are legitimate targets since by their presence there, they are guilty of aggression against the dar al-islam. Thus, according to this rationale, to bomb an Israeli shopping mall, restaurant, or even school bus is not an attack on innocent noncombatants but an attack on people who, by being where they are, are taking part in the ongoing aggression against the dar al-islam.

Such reasoning significantly extends and distorts the original—and still normative—meaning of defensive jihad. It is no great step, although still a significant one, to the justification al Qaeda's spokesmen have given for its campaign of terrorism.

## THE IDEA OF JIHAD ACCORDING TO OSAMA BIN LADEN

In February 1998, styling himself as "Shaykh," Osama bin Laden, together with several associates, all leaders of violent, radical Islamist groups in various countries (one was Ayman al-Zawahiri, who has since emerged as bin Laden's closest lieutenant), issued a fatwa, or formal religious interpretive ruling, calling for jihad against "the crusader-Zionist alliance." The fatwa, issued under the title "World Islamic Front Statement Urging Jihad against Jews and Crusaders," included the following statement:

> In compliance with God's order, we issue the following fatwa to all Muslims: The ruling to kill the Americans and their allies—civilians and military—is an individual duty for every Muslim who can do it in any country in which it is possible to do it, in order to liberate the al-Aqsa Mosque [Jerusalem] and the holy mosque [Mecca] from their grip, and in order for their armies to move out of the lands of Islam. . . . This is in accordance with the words of Almighty God, "and fight the pagans all together as they fight you all together," and "fight them until there is no more tumult or oppression, and there prevail justice and faith in God."

While bin Laden, Zawahiri, and others speaking on behalf of al Qaeda have issued various other statements since the September 11 attacks (and continue to do so), this fatwa stands as a fundamental statement of the terrorist rationale: an appeal to the Islamic tradition of emergency defensive jihad by which every Muslim is obligated, as an individual duty, to take up arms against the invaders from the territory of war, or dar al-harb. Mainstream Muslim scholars up to and including the current Shaykh al-Azhar, the head of the preeminent faculty of Islamic law in the world, have declared that bin Laden and his associates here use this traditional idea in a way that distorts its meaning and is invalid as a guide for behavior. Yet, it remains a powerful statement, employing a well-recognized form of religious judgment to evoke the deep tradition of the jihad of individual duty to justify and rationalize universal, unlimited warfare against all Americans, that is to say, a universal campaign employing terrorist means and recognizing no limits. What are the religious elements of this effort at justification?

The first is its form as a fatwa, a juristic ruling on a matter of binding Islamic law. A fatwa properly is a collective ruling by a group of scholars (*fuqaha*) trained in *fiqh*, Islamic jurisprudence. It follows certain stylistic conventions: a question posed, the ruling in answer to the question, supporting references to the Qur'an, and further references to earlier opinions and rulings by other authorities on *fiqh*. The 1998 statement follows these stylistic conventions point by point. What is wrong, though, is that bin Laden and his associates have no credentials as *fuqaha*; they are all leaders of violent, radical Islamist groups, with various levels of formal education in various fields, but none is a scholar of *fiqh*.

The second is the distortion of the juristic tradition on the jihad of individual duty. The classical juristic conception did not envision such jihad as a permanent replacement for the jihad of collective duty but as a short-term response to an immediate emergency, to be abandoned once the immediate emergency was past. The emergency, moreover, was understood as a military invasion. The statement from bin Laden and his associates, by contrast, postulates a broad and continuing state of emergency, vaguely defined in terms of the presence of non-Islamic powers and influence. It is not a short-term response to the immediate emergency caused by a military invasion but rather a call to jihad that turns it into a conflict of cultures. It is difficult to know when this emergency will end, short of the eschatological triumph of the dar al-islam over all non-Muslim societies throughout the world. Clearly, in terms of the question whether the war against terrorism is a conflict of cultures, the answer given here, from the side of the terrorists, is yes.

Several additional distortions of the normative tradition on jihad of the sword may be identified. A fundamental one is this conception's understanding of any territory that was once under Muslim rule as land properly belonging to the dar al-islam. The growth of the dar al-islam, thus, can go only one way; since, by Islamic eschatology, it is destined to encompass the world, it can only expand, not shrink. The second distortion is the concept of the proper rule of such territory: it cannot be ruled by a non-Islamic government or its proxy, whether the latter be a colonial government or a westernizing ruler like Anwar Sadat or the last shah of Iran. Contemporary Muslim rulers, thus, must take care not to seem too pro-Western as this may make them targets for overthrow by radical Islamists. The third distortion is the requirement that such a society be governed by a strict interpretation of Islamic law, the sharia, and such law only. The statement by bin Laden and his associates, thus, clearly carries still further the lines of development identified in earlier radical Islamist movements, which adapted the concept of the jihad of individual duty to their own ends.

This reconception of the idea of defensive jihad is a harsh one, one that leads to a rejection of much of the actual history of Muslim societies and of Muslim faith. It leaves scant room for toleration of the "people of the book," as prescribed in the Qur'an, because under the extended definition of what constitutes an aggression against the dar al-islam, Jews and Christians present in dominantly Muslim societies become assimilated to this aggression. Because the view of what is properly Muslim is so restricted, the manager of a Western chain store or restaurant catering to Westerners becomes defined as one taking part in the aggression, guilty of subverting Islamic values. This extension of the idea of defensive jihad also leads to intolerance against Muslims who think differently. It leaves no room for difference of interpretation as to what Islam requires; its reading of the sharia is narrow and unyielding on doctrine and behavior alike. Social developments identified with modernity are rejected as un-Islamic, despite the fact that large numbers of Muslims have adopted them without losing their faith. Even more deeply, this expanded idea of defensive jihad is deeply revolutionary in its implications for Islamic societies. Not only does it implicitly target many of their leaders, but it also undermines the social structures and relationships on which organized society rests, for in the face of the declared situation of emergency, all such structures and relationships, from family to school to workplace to government, are redefined by the degree to which they support jihad. Finally, the claim of an emergency situation in which all of the rules of restraint no longer apply leads directly to the phenomenon we recognize as terrorism: attacks figuratively or literally out of the blue on ordinary people going about their everyday lives for the purpose of sowing terror among other ordinary people as a means of influencing their government's decisions.

The fundamental justification of defensive jihad cited by bin Laden and his associates is that since the Gulf War, the United States has been militarily "occupying the lands of Islam in the holiest of places, the Arabian Peninsula"; that is, the presence of U.S. military personnel and matériel in Saudi Arabia, although present there with the consent of the Saudi government, constitutes aggression against the dar al-islam. The 1998 fatwa also cites two further forms of aggression: the "protracted blockade" against Iraq and the aim "to serve the Jews' petty state and divert attention from its occupation of Jerusalem and murder of Muslims there." So, the United States, the embodiment of the dar al-harb, is engaged in aggression against the dar al-islam. This is the same sort of extension—and distortion—of the normative idea of defensive jihad as found in the reasoning discussed earlier. Bin Laden's statement goes still further, however, in the judgment that this justifies any and all Muslims "who can do it" in killing any and all Americans, "civilians and military" alike, "in any country in which it is possible to do it." This is not defensive war any longer; it is offensive warfare, taking the battle to the homeland of the nation deemed guilty of aggression.

Bin Laden, of course, by normative Islamic tradition, lacks the religiopolitical authority necessary to initiate such offensive war as he is not a designated heir to the ruling authority of the Prophet. Thus, he has to describe his war against America as defensive and not offensive. By painting all Americans as equally guilty of the "aggression" identified, he also sets aside the limits imposed on warfare by normative Islamic tradition: no direct, intended killing of noncombatants and no use of fire, the weapon prohibited for Muslim use in offense because it is the weapon God will use in the last days. In his description of the situation, there are no noncombatants; Americans are all aggressors. And Americans have used fire against the dar al-islam in the war with Iraq, so it may now be used against Americans.

The traditional, normative conception of defensive jihad is still visible through bin Laden's reasoning, but its meaning has been distorted into a doctrine far removed from what the jurists who first formulated it had in mind and transformed into something they sought to make illegitimate: a justification for the waging of war nominally on behalf of the Islamic community but in fact by private individuals for their own goals. One can probably call al Qaeda's war against America and the West a holy war on its own terms, but it is emphatically not the striving in the path of God required by the normative Islamic conception of defensive jihad.

## RESPONDING JUSTLY: THE OBLIGATIONS OF A MORAL RESPONSE TO TERRORISM

Thinking about the moral dimensions of our response to terrorism means, in one way or another, that we need to think about the evil that has been done and our obligations in responding to it in terms of the just war tradition. This tradition has represented the main line of Western culture's thinking about war and violence since it first came together as a coherent body of thought and practice in the Middle Ages, and the tradition's presence and influence runs deep in normative thought on war in Western culture and, particularly, in American reflection on the moral use of military force. Although it has deep religious roots, and although there are specifically religious versions of it in use in contemporary moral reflection on war, this is emphatically not a tradition of holy war, war justified by religious cause and religious authority and fought accordingly. Rather, normative just war thinking developed historically in such a way as to repudiate such war for religion, instead defining the justified use of armed force in terms of the moral parameters of the protection of the good of the political community. Today, the just war tradition is deeply imbedded in international law, particularly in the law of armed conflict, and just war thinking has an important presence in American thought within the religious, academic, and policy spheres. It has had an especially important influence within the sphere of military life, where the idea of just war today appears in the curricula of the service academies and the various war colleges, is treated in the centers for military ethics associated with the service academies, is addressed in special conferences, and is taken seriously in the interpretation of the law, both domestic and international, relating to armed conflict. Indeed, although not too recently just war thinking was primarily found in the academic world or in the religious spheres and their involvement in policy debate, today some of the most sustained and serious engagement with the moral requirements for the use of armed force found in this tradition is in the American military. That, I think, has obvious implications for assessing the moral nature of our military response to terrorism, as well as the broader question of how we should think about the peace we hope to secure by defeating terror.

It is usual to speak of the just war idea as having two aspects: one, the *jus ad bellum*, having to do with whether military force is justified in a given circumstance, and two, the *jus in bello*, having to do with the moral restraints to be observed in using justified force. Historically and thematically, the core of the jus ad bellum is constituted by four requirements: that the use of force be undertaken by a sovereign authority, for a just cause, with right intention, and with the end of restoring peace. These are all deontological in nature; that is, they express moral duties. In recent just war thinking, three prudential concerns are usually attached to them, further qualifying the right to use justified force in any particular case: that the resort to force be expected to bring more good than harm (the idea of proportionality), that it be expected to succeed in its aims (the idea of reasonable hope of success), and that no other means are likely to secure what the use of force is expected to secure (the idea of last resort). While much recent just war debate has focused on these three prudential concerns, historically and thematically, they play a secondary role in the moral determination of whether a use of force is just or not; the four deontological criteria—sovereign authority, just cause, right intention, and the aim of peace—are the core concerns. One prominent contemporary version of just war thinking, that of the U.S. Catholic bishops (which I treat further below), defines the idea of just war as beginning with a "presumption against war," so that the principles defining just war exist simply to provide exceptions to the general rule of avoidance of armed force. But one does not find this understanding in historical just war tradition. Rather, the fundamental problem, as this tradition rightly understood has it, is that just societies must sometimes employ force to protect themselves, their citizens, and the ideals of justice on which those societies depend, as well as the broader structure of international relations in which just societies coexist, against evil and the threat of evil directed at them. The traditional formulation of the idea of just cause puts this succinctly: there are three such causes—defense against attack, recovery of that which has been wrongly taken, and punishment of evil. These causes, when they exist, come upon the just society from outside; they are genuine expressions of wrongdoing. Faced with them, singly or all together, it is a responsibility of just government to respond; doing so is its moral obligation. The government that does not do so is simply not, in moral terms, doing its duty.

So, the just war tradition is first and foremost about the place that the use of force may have in the exercise of the responsibilities of good government—the "sovereign authority," in the language of the tradition. These are positive responsibilities: to ensure the common good, to protect against threats, and to support the order that makes just societies possible. In the specific, and very simple, terms of the Augustinian language used in medieval formulations of the idea of just war, the sovereign authority is to provide a just and peaceful social order. The responsibility to serve order, justice, and peace is not at odds with the use of force on behalf of the society; rather, force is a tool that societies must sometimes use to attain those goods of order, justice, and peace.

It is through this prism that we should regard the just war requirement that the use of armed force should serve the end of peace. Doing so is what good government is fundamentally about; not doing so betrays the public good itself. It is also through this prism that we should read the just war requirement of right intention, classically put in Augustine's listing of various sorts of wrong intentions, including the love of power, the desire to dominate utterly, a "lust for vengeance," and an "implacable animosity." In Augustine's terms, these are all personal sins: a sovereign or an individual soldier who takes up arms motivated by them is guilty of selfish motivation and does not strive to serve the cause of justice, peace, and a stable human order. There is an interesting insight here: just as those in authority may sometimes be responsible for using force on behalf of their societies to protect and serve the justice, peace, and order found there, so the presence of wrong intention makes the use of force something else—a vendetta, an act of injustice itself.

In the historical development of the just war tradition, the idea of noncombatant immunity is tied to this requirement of right intention in the use of force, and in the contemporary context, it finds expression in the idea that it is always wrong to target people because of their ethnicity, tribal or clan membership, or religious or other beliefs. Let me for a moment recall Osama bin Laden's fatwa, calling on "every Muslim who can do it" to "kill the Americans and their allies" "in any country in which it is possible to do it." I commented earlier on the problematic nature of this fatwa in terms of the Islamic religious tradition; now let me note that these words in particular express something directly opposite to the moral requirements for the use of force according to the idea of just war. Bin Laden calls for killing "Americans and their allies" in general, and we have seen directly what this means in the attacks on ordinary civilians going about their daily work on September 11, 2001. Who is to do it? Not a sovereign authority acting on behalf of a just social order in response to harm done to it, but every individual Muslim who can do it out of a state of implacable animosity toward those targeted. Again, this is precisely what the justified use of force is not. In using force against the terror of bin Laden and al Qaeda, we may use the example of the great wrong that they have done to remind us of how to fight against them rightly.

I have already slipped into discussion of the jus in bello, the moral restraints to be observed in using justified force. Now let me briefly treat it more directly. While most recent moral discourse describes the jus in bello in terms of two moral principles, discrimination and proportionality, these terms originated only forty years ago in Paul Ramsey's thought. Historically, the just war tradition did not use these terms or think about right use of force in this way. On noncombatant immunity, the approach was to disallow direct, intended attacks on people who, because of certain personal characteristics or their function in society, did not bear arms or directly support those who did; that is, the traditional approach was to define as noncombatants such groups as children, women, the aged, workers of all sorts going about their civilian occupations, the clergy, peaceful travelers, and so on. When a rationale was given, it was simply this: these do not make war; so they should not have war made against them. If individuals from these groups crossed the line into functional participation in the conflict, then they might be targeted; still, though, the groups themselves were to be protected and allowed so far as possible to go about their ordinary lives. This is still the approach taken in the international law of armed conflict. It has the advantage of clarity: unless you have a good reason to think otherwise, you have no right to directly, intentionally target people like this. How different this way of thinking is from that of contemporary terrorism, which directly and intentionally targets precisely such people going about their everyday lives in the most ordinary ways.

On the matter of the means of war, traditional just war thinking, like the contemporary law of armed conflicts, sought to impose limits by banning certain weapons as bad in themselves (for example, weapons of mass destruction in today's law of armed conflict) or as bad when used in particular ways (for example, bombardment of undefended places or intentional destruction of crops or means of transportation).

In the military response to terrorism, the implications of moral limits on the means of war may suggestively be examined by reflection on the capabilities and use of precision-guided munitions (PGMs). Avoidance of both harm to noncombatants and unnecessary destruction is served by the use of weapons that can be laid on their proper target with a high and consistent level of accuracy, a capability that in turn allows for the use of fewer weapons and weapons of lower destructive yield on any given target. In simple and straightforward terms, this profoundly changes the calculus of discrimination and proportionality within conflict. The concept of "collateral damage" refers to unintended harm to people and property in the immediate area of a proper target that is the object of a strike. If one cannot be sure of hitting the desired target with one warhead, then many warheads have to be used; if one cannot be sure of striking close enough to the desired target to destroy it, then more destructive warheads have to be used. In moral terms, one quickly enters the realm of the rule of double effect when thinking about the collateral harm done by weapons aimed at a proper target but incapable of hitting it accurately. PGMs change this. We have seen the results, increasingly, in the Gulf War and in the air strikes over Kosovo and, more recently, in the conduct of the war against al Qaeda and their Taliban supporters in Afghanistan, where it is reported that 60 percent or more of all air strikes used PGMs, and in Operation Iraqi Freedom, which I will discuss further below.

To look more closely at the case of Afghanistan, critics of the use of military force there (to be sure, there were not many) called up the vision of "carpet bombing," of the destruction of Afghan cities and towns to rubble and of massive casualties among ordinary Afghan civilians. The reality was strikingly different: while strikes did occur within Afghan cities and towns, they were against specific targets identified as legitimate, and both the collateral damage and the unintended damage (as from a missile or a bomb going off course) were limited. But relatively few strikes in fact took place within Afghan population centers. Instead, heavy bombers armed with JDAM technology became weapons of choice for bombardment of Taliban positions, first in the front lines outside Kabul, and more recently in the eastern mountains campaigns. Not only cruise missiles but missiles fired from robotic drones have proved themselves as PGMs against smaller targets.

Now, why is this morally significant? The answer is, because PGMs give the American military (and at this point only the American military) the ability to fight in the way moralists have long been saying they should fight: in a way that avoids harm to noncombatants and minimizes overall destruction to the society which, after the war is over, must be brought back to a state of peace. Anyone who has followed the American moral debate over military force for the last forty or so years knows that a recurrent theme among opponents of military force has been that, in the contemporary age, war is inherently indiscriminate and disproportionately destructive and that any use of military force is accordingly questionable. This thinking was, for example, in the background of the U.S. Catholic bishops' idea of a "presumption against war," and it remains the rationale for such a presumption in the thought of prominent Catholic just war thinker Bryan Hehir. The conception of contemporary war as inherently indiscriminate and disproportionate also played a prominent role in the argument of the bishops of the United Methodist Church in their pastoral statement *In Defense of Creation* (1986). It was a prominent feature in the National Council of Churches' opposition to the use of force to roll back Iraqi aggression at the time of the Gulf War. And, of course, this was also one of the lines of argument used by critics of U.S. military action in Afghanistan and, as we shall see, in Iraq against the Saddam Hussein regime. My point is simple and to the contrary: Contemporary war is not inherently indiscriminate or grossly destructive. It is not by necessity nuclear war or even warfare characterized by World War II–type strategic bombing. The use of military force does not, because of some inherent law, escalate to such levels or "spin out of control," as one critic of the Gulf War put it. Rather, PGMs provide a vastly increased operational capability to fight according to the moral requirements of the just war idea.

The morality or immorality of any use of armed force is, finally, not mainly a matter of the kind of force available but of who uses it, why, and how. This is ultimately the difference between the terrorist attacks of September 11 and the American military response against the Taliban and al Qaeda. Nonetheless, given that the use is justified, then there is a moral obligation to avoid harm to those who ought not be targeted and to seek to minimize the total destruction that the use of force brings about. That is where the operational capabilities of PGMs are morally important. There are those who worry that the possession of PGMs will in the future tempt American presidents to resort to their use more easily, when other means short of force would be better. That may be, but that is a different kind of moral issue to be addressed on its own terms by other means. From my perspective, it is far more important that an American president, having determined that there is a moral obligation to use force to protect the American people and defend the international order, should have the most moral means at his disposal to do so. That is, I suggest, what we have seen in the war against al Qaeda and the Taliban in Afghanistan, and it shows what military resources we are able to apply to the further war on terrorism.

Let me conclude this introductory look at the idea of just war and the tradition out of which it has come by again drawing attention to the aim of war, according to this tradition: to establish or restore peace. A classic statement of this end is provided by the words of Augustine: "We do not seek peace in order to be at war, but we go to war that we may have peace. Be peaceful, therefore, in warring, so that you may vanquish those whom you war against and bring them to the prosperity of peace" (*Augustine, Letter clxxxix*). As noted briefly earlier, within the frame of the Augustinian conception of politics in which the just war tradition is rooted, the good society is one characterized by order, justice, and peace. But although each of these expresses a distinctive aspect of the whole, they are linked together: a good order is one that is just and peaceful; justice implies a right ordering of relationships within the society, thus there is peace among its members; and the good of peace thus includes the requirements of right order and justice. Unpacking these two characteristics further, Americans would insist that a rightly ordered and just society—thus one at peace within itself and open to peace with other societies as well—is one whose people have personal freedom and whose government is democratic. Even more broadly, to fight justly means to aim at protecting and preserving all those values that underwrite this sacred conception of peace. The just war tradition does not end with how it justifies armed force or with the limits it places on employing such force, but with the aim at which justified resort to force must always aim: to establish or restore peace. A just war against terror, then, is not simply about the right, even the obligation, to use armed force to protect our selves, our society, and the values we cherish; it is not only about how we should fight in this cause; it is ultimately about the peace we seek to establish in contrast to the war that the terrorists have set in motion. We are, as Augustine put it, to "be peaceful . . . in warring," that is, to keep the aim of peace first and foremost, and not only to "vanquish those whom you war against" but also to "bring them to the prosperity of peace." The peace described here is a peace in which all may share. Just war responds to enmity, but it seeks to overcome enmity in the end. The ideal expressed in the just war tradition is far from a celebration of wrath, violence, and enmity; it is an ideal in which the use of force serves to overcome these and to create peace. This is a purpose that must not be forgotten.

# 2

# DISCIPLINING JUST WAR THINKING

## Uses and Misuses of the Just War Idea in Recent American Debate

I n the previous chapter, I briefly described the origins, historical development, and classic form of the just war idea as defining a tradition that is deeply embedded in Western moral thinking about the use of armed force. In that context, I also mentioned, in order to criticize them, two prominent contemporary examples of religious conceptions of just war: those found in official statements of the U.S. Catholic bishops and of the United Methodist bishops. These two conceptions of the content and implications of the idea of just war differ markedly from each other, and both differ importantly from the classic conception found in historical just war tradition. In fact, the recent recovery of the idea of just war and its use in debate over specific uses of American armed force has produced an even greater variety of versions of the just war idea. Claims made on behalf of appeals to the idea of just war vary accordingly. I aim in this chapter to lay out some of the most prominent contemporary versions of just war thinking so as to be able to think critically about them and the arguments put forward on their basis. In the following chapter, I look specifically at several important uses of the just war idea in the debate over whether to use force to oust Saddam Hussein. The present chapter, then, examines the conceptual context out of which these arguments come.

### AN EARLY BENCHMARK: PAUL RAMSEY ON JUST WAR

It is helpful to begin at the beginning of the recovery of the just war idea in recent American thought, that is, with the conception of just war put forward by the individual who effectively began that recovery. This was Protestant theologian Paul Ramsey, who in two books published in the 1960s, *War and the Christian Conscience* (1961) and *The Just War* (1968), defined a conception of just war centered on two moral principles, discrimination and proportionality. These are, of course, moral principles addressing right conduct in the use of armed force, and his choice to focus on them importantly reflected the specific context that shaped Ramsey's thought in this period: the debate over nuclear strategy, over possible tactical uses of nuclear weapons, and toward the end of the decade, over the conduct of the war in Vietnam. But Ramsey also focused on the question of moral conduct in the use of military force because he regarded the choice of whether to resort to military force as belonging to the exercise of statecraft, in which, he believed, moralists might advise but had no competence to decide. Matters of right conduct in the use of force, by contrast, have to do directly with the individual conscience of soldiers and citizens, and here the moralist has something to say. A third factor, substantively the most important, was the centrality of the idea of love in Christian ethical thought during the 1960s, a factor that clearly influenced the sources he turned to for the idea of just war and the way he interpreted them.

The fundamental moral question, for Ramsey, was that which he asked as the subtitle to *War and the Christian Conscience: How Shall Modern War Be Conducted Justly?* His answer looked to the requirements of love of neighbor as he read these out of the New Testament and found them expressed particularly in the thought of Augustine. Love of neighbor, Ramsey argued, is the source of the permission, and sometimes the obligation, to use force to protect that neighbor when wrongly threatened. At the same time, love of the guilty assailant requires that no more force than necessary be used against the guilty while protecting the innocent. These two concerns—permission with limitation—are always present, Ramsey argued, and they lead directly to the two moral principles for right conduct in the use of force, discrimination and proportionality. Discrimination means that one may never use force against the innocent, while proportionality means that even the force used against the guilty must be no more than required to attain the justified end. Love of neighbor is the driving concern in both cases. Love establishes the principle of discrimination as an exceptionless moral rule. The principle of proportionality, by contrast, requires moral calculation that must be guided by love for the two different sorts of neighbors in question. The core elements of Ramsey's conception of just war are summarized in figure 2.1.

Ramsey went on to develop an important addition to his understanding of discrimination. Sometimes, in seeking to protect the innocent, one may inad-

**Figure 2.1  Paul Ramsey on Just War**

Love of neighbor and the Christian use of force:
- Love of the innocent neighbor as the source of permission and sometimes obligation to use force to protect that neighbor
- Love of the guilty neighbor as the source of the obligation to use no more force than necessary against the guilty while protecting the innocent

Jus in bello principles:
- *Discrimination:* the obligation never to use force against the innocent directly and intentionally
- *Proportionality:* the obligation to use no more force than necessary to achieve the end

The rule of double effect:
- One may never directly and intentionally do harm to an innocent person; yet, because a good act may have bad effects, it is allowable to harm innocents indirectly and unintentionally when directly and intentionally aiming at a legitimate target.

vertently harm them. Is one then guilty for that harm? Ramsey found the answer to this problem in the rule of double effect as he found it in Aquinas: moral guilt follows from direct, intended wrong action, not from actions directed and intended to do good which, as secondary and unintended effects, also do harm. Thus, his final phrasing of the principle of discrimination was that one may never directly and intentionally use force against the innocent; this is the exceptionless moral rule. But this phrasing also required a broadening out of the implications of proportionality: first understood as applying only to the level of harm that could be directed to the guilty assailant, it now bears also on determining when and whether one may use a particular kind of force, or indeed any force at all, to protect the innocent, as that force may produce secondary, unintended (collateral) harm to the innocent, and one must weigh that in terms of a calculus of proportionality.

Ramsey himself clearly thought that there are times when the obligation to defend the neighbor from harm justifies the use of force and may even oblige it. Thus, for example, he argued for the morality of counterforce targeting of nuclear weapons, even taking into account the possibility of collateral damage, and at the beginning of the American involvement in Vietnam, he laid out in just war terms a forceful argument for intervention on behalf of the South Vietnamese. Clearly, he had a conception of a *jus ad bellum*, even if he avoided developing one systematically. But from the perspective of later debate, what has proven most durable is his stress on the requirements of the *jus in bello*.

Without a formal jus ad bellum, later writers have often turned his principles of discrimination and proportionality into a form of jus ad bellum, or rather, what Ramsey, opposing this line of argument, called a *jus contra bellum jus-tum*. According to this argument, if noncombatants are expected to suffer, particularly if heavy damage to noncombatant life is expected to follow from a use of armed force, then that use cannot be justified. Ramsey's careful consideration of the difference between direct and intended harm to noncombatants and indirect, unintended harm is forgotten here. Also, proportionality in this argument is not a calculation of good versus bad effects but a judgment that heavy damage is inherently disproportionate. Although Ramsey himself understood his conception of just war to amount to a moral refutation of the claims of pacifism, this later interpretation of his argument made it over into a form of pacifist rejection of contemporary warfare. This argument, though, was not a form of absolute pacifism but a new expression of modern-war pacifism, an idea dating to the rise of modern warfare in the nineteenth century, which holds that the destructiveness of modern war is inevitably so great as to be disproportionate to any goods sought and that noncombatant life is always going to bear the brunt of the suffering. In the debate of the 1960s, such modern-war pacifism took the particular form of nuclear pacifism, the rejection of any use of nuclear weapons in war as inherently indiscriminate and disproportionate. Although Ramsey was himself opposed to this view, use of his conception of just war to support it has been an unfortunate legacy of his contribution to the recovery of just war thinking in American moral debate. Using jus in bello principles to argue against a jus ad bellum has become, as we shall see in the case of the American Catholic bishops in the next section, a feature of arguments that use just war language to oppose resort to armed force.

## THE CATHOLIC BISHOPS ON JUST WAR

Another important benchmark in the development of contemporary conceptions of just war was the publication of the U.S. Catholic bishops' pastoral letter, *The Challenge of Peace*, in 1983. Their description of the just war idea is summarized in figure 2.2. It made several important departures from the classic just war tradition.

First, *The Challenge of Peace* described Catholic just war doctrine as beginning with a general "presumption against war" and represented the jus ad bellum criteria as guidance for determining whether this presumption should be overruled in particular cases or not. The classical tradition, by contrast,

**Figure 2.2   The Just War Criteria as Defined by the U.S. Catholic Bishops:** *The Challenge of Peace* **(1983)**

**Presupposition:** There is a "presumption against war."

**Jus ad bellum:**

**Just cause:**
To confront "a real and certain danger"
To protect innocent life
To preserve conditions necessary for decent human existence
To secure basic human rights

**Competent authority:**
"In the Catholic tradition the use of force has always been joined to the common good: war must be declared by those with responsibility for public order."

**Comparative justice:**
Relative levels of right on both sides of a dispute; whether sufficient right exists to override the presumption against war

**Right intention:**
"War can be initiated only for the reasons set forth above as a just cause." During conflict, pursuit of peace and reconciliation, avoidance of unnecessary destruction, unreasonable conditions.

**Last resort:**
"For resort to war to be justified, all reasonable alternatives must have been exhausted."

**Probability of success:**
No use of force when the outcome will be "either disproportionate or futile"; yet "at times defense of key values, even against great odds, may be a 'proportionate' witness."

**Proportionality:**
"The damage to be inflicted and the costs incurred by war must be proportionate to the good expected by taking up arms."

**Jus in bello:**

**Proportionality:**
Avoidance of "escalation to broader or total war" or "to the use of weapons of horrendous destructive potential."

**Discrimination:**
"The principle prohibits directly intended attacks on non-combatants and non-military targets."

had thought of the use of force as morally neutral, good when a war was determined to be just (*justum bellum*), a use of force by the sovereign authority of a political community for a just cause, rather narrowly defined, and with a right intention, defined negatively as the avoidance of a number of wrong motives, including self-aggrandizement, theft, bullying, and action out of hatred of the other simply for being the other, and defined positively as intended to establish or restore peace. To cast the just war idea as beginning with a general presumption against war was to make it into something different from what the classic idea had been. Where did this new conception of just war come from? First, it reflected the context in which *The Challenge of Peace* appeared: the debate over nuclear weapons and mutual assured destruction during the buildup of nuclear arms undertaken by the Reagan administration. The presumption against war was a way of giving force to the Catholic bishops' opposition to the use of nuclear weapons under any circumstances. Second, the presumption against war conception reflected the presence on the drafting committee for the pastoral letter, as well as among the bishops more generally and among the Catholic faithful, of a strong pacifist sentiment. This was often put in terms of the teaching of Vatican II that the spirituality of those in religious life should be expanded also among the laity and among secular clergy; the pacifism of those in religious life was thus extended into a claim that pacifism should be an option for all Catholics. The presumption against war idea provided a middle ground on which those who favored a just war approach and the pacifists could come together: both shared that presumption. A question, of course, is whether the just war proponents here did not give up too much, making the idea of just war over into a position effectively pacifist in practice. But the deeper question is whether the result was faithful to the classic idea of just war at all. The third source of the presumption against war conception of the just war idea was a 1978 article in the Jesuit journal *Theological Studies* by academic ethicist James F. Childress. In this article, Childress undertook to develop a contemporary concept of just war based on the moral ideal of nonmaleficence, following the model of an ethic of prima facie duties as outlined by the philosopher W. D. Ross. Childress argued here that the killing and harm done in war is inherently morally problematic; it is prima facie wrong to injure or kill others. To do so, justification is needed to overrule this prima facie presumption against war. The just war criteria provide this justification. The structure of the idea of just war as defined in *The Challenge of Peace* followed Childress's conception closely. While this was an interesting thought experiment, useful if there had been no historical just war tradition to draw from, the resulting concept diverged importantly from that tradition, and so did the version of it found in *The Challenge of Peace*.

Several other notable changes from the classic just war idea need to be noted. First, *The Challenge of Peace* gave primacy of place to the requirement of just cause, whereas the classic tradition had always given priority to the requirement of sovereign authority because only such authority has responsibility for the common good, which the use of force may be needed to protect. What the bishops called "competent authority," which refers to its legal status rather than the moral responsibility of political leadership, they placed second after the requirement of just cause. Who, in this conception, gets to determine whether there is just cause for use of force, if not the person or people in sovereign authority? Perhaps the bishops themselves, or at any rate the moralists, rather than the political leadership, despite the fact that the bishops and the moralists have no responsibility for such leadership and the outcome of whatever decision they may make. A second change was the addition to the jus ad bellum of the requirement of comparative justice, that the relative levels of right and wrong on both sides of a dispute should be weighed, as well as three new consequentialist criteria, last resort, probability of success, and overall proportionality, all strengthening the presumption against war. Arguably important elements for the responsible exercise of governing authority in general, these had never been listed as specific elements of the just war idea in earlier just war thought. Subsequent usage has often treated these new prudential criteria as the most important, and they have repeatedly been interpreted by reference to worst-possible-case claims about the bad outcomes to be expected from a use of armed force. This was certainly the case in the debate of 2002–2003, as it had been in the Catholic bishops' official statements opposing the use of force to remove Iraq from Kuwait after Iraq's aggressive conquest and annexation of that country in 1990. A third change from the classic definition of just war, one whose importance cannot be understated, was the entire omission of the requirement that a just resort to armed force must aim at peace. I have often wondered why the aim of peace was left out of the just war jus ad bellum as stated by *The Challenge of Peace*: I think it is because once one has begun by describing war as always something negative, it is conceptually impossible to represent it as a way to peace. This is profoundly different from the sensibility expressed in classic just war thought, where armed force is a tool that may be used for good or ill and where the assumption was not "against war" but against the evil and injustice that unfortunately abound in the affairs of men and nations, which armed force may be required to remedy. Augustine explained the end of peace in these terms: "We do not seek peace in order to be at war, but we go to war that we may have peace." This is an idea entirely lacking in *The Challenge of Peace*, which frames peace wholly in terms of the absence of war, despite the threats to peace that may remain.

In 1993, the Catholic bishops issued a new statement about war and peace, marking the ten-year anniversary of the earlier pastoral letter, and in it they adopted a slightly different description of the idea of just war (figure 2.3). The presumption against war here became "a strong presumption against the use of force" (*Harvest of Justice*, 5–6). The requirement of comparative justice was placed second in the new listing of jus ad bellum requirements, demoting

**Figure 2.3   The Just War Criteria as Defined by the U.S. Catholic Bishops: "The Harvest of Justice Is Sown in Peace" (1993).**

**Presupposition:** "The just-war tradition begins with a strong presumption against the use of force and then establishes the conditions when this presumption may be overridden for the sake of preserving the kind of peace which protects human dignity and human rights."

**Jus ad bellum:**

**Just cause:**
"Force may be used only to correct a grave, public evil, i.e., aggression or massive violation of the basic rights of whole populations."

**Comparative justice:**
"To override the presumption against the use of force the injustice suffered by one party must significantly outweigh that suffered by the other."

**Legitimate authority:**
"Only duly constituted public authorities may use deadly force or wage war."

**Right intention:**
"Force may be used only in a truly just cause and solely for that purpose."

**Probability of success:**
"Arms may not be used in a futile cause or in a case where disproportionate measures are required to achieve success."

**Proportionality:**
"The overall destruction expected from the use of force must be outweighed by the good to be achieved."

**Last resort:**
"Force may be used only after all peaceful alternatives have been seriously tried and exhausted."

**Jus in bello:**

**Noncombatant immunity:**
"Civilians may not be the object of direct attack, and military personnel must take due care to avoid and minimize indirect harm to civilians."

**Proportionality:**
"Efforts must be made to attain military objectives with no more force than is militarily necessary and to avoid disproportionate collateral damage to civilian life and property."

**Right intention:**
"The aim . . . must be peace with justice, so that acts of vengeance and indiscriminate violence . . . are forbidden."

what was now called "legitimate authority" (further emphasizing the legal status of governing authority over against the moral responsibility of government) to third place. The 1993 statement did mention the aim of peace, but incomprehensibly, it set this as a requirement of the jus in bello, making it not a concern to be satisfied when deciding whether resort to force will be justified but only after one has engaged in using force. In the 1993 statement, the aim of peace is stated so as to reinforce the requirements of discrimination and proportionality, explicitly forbidding "acts of vengeance and indiscriminate violence." No one can quarrel with this as a restriction to be observed in the moral conduct of war; yet, I believe the classic just war tradition had it right in placing this consideration as one to be held in mind in deciding whether to use force in the first place. This is effectively what the classic tradition meant by right intention, understood as the avoiding of wrong intentions. By contrast, both *The Challenge of Peace* and the bishops' statement of ten years later offered only a thin, essentially vacuous, description of the criterion of right intention: the intention must be in accord with the just cause.

In practice, statements from representatives of the U.S. Conference of Catholic Bishops have deviated somewhat from both of the listings of just war criteria that I have just discussed. In November 2002, the U.S. Conference of Catholic Bishops issued a statement on Iraq, which, after beginning by defining just war reasoning as defining "strict conditions for overriding the strong presumption against military force," included only four of the earlier named jus ad bellum criteria—just cause, legitimate authority, probability of success, and proportionality—while citing the two jus in bello principles of "civilian immunity and proportionality" as further concerns to be met in the decision to initiate use of armed force. Each of these criteria was accompanied by a paragraph defining what the bishops believed it required in the situation being addressed. The discussion of just cause singled out as wrong "preventive uses of military force to overthrow threatening regimes or to deal with weapons of mass destruction." Here, the question of preemptive use of force was rephrased more negatively as preventive use of force. The bishops also rejected the aim of ending a government's "existence" as opposed to changing "unacceptable behavior." The statement interpreted the criterion of legitimate authority to require not only compliance with U.S. constitutional standards and broad national consensus but also "some form of international sanction," which was then rephrased as action taking place "within the framework of the United Nations." Here the traditional concept of sovereign authority as responsibility for the common good of the political community has been restated as the concept of legitimacy (that is, legality) within the frame of the U.N. system. The bishops used their interpretation of the prudential criteria of probability of success and proportionality to voice their judgment that "war against Iraq might have unpredictable consequences," echoing judgments made nine years earlier to oppose military efforts to expel Iraqi forces from Kuwait after Iraq's invasion and occupation of that country. The discussion of "civilian immunity" and proportionality in the in bello sense was used effectively as a further jus ad bellum criterion, with the treatment of proportionality in the two contexts elided together. Again, the thrust of the statement's discussion here was to state the bishops' judgment that "the use of military force in Iraq could bring incalculable costs for a civilian population." In short, the bishops used this statement to reject preemption and regime change, not discussing any other justifications the Bush administration had offered, to stress the legal necessity of a U.N. sanction for military action, and to offer the judgment that military force could not be used against Iraq without indiscriminate and disproportionate destruction. Nothing was said about the other just war criteria or about how the definitions offered in this statement related to those given in the 1983 and 1993 statements or to those found in the classic just war tradition.

This 2002 statement grew out of a letter to President Bush of earlier that fall from Bishop Wilton Gregory, president of the U.S. Conference of Catholic Bishops. I examine that letter in detail in chapter 3 as an important early entry into just war debate over the question of the use of force against Iraq. Gregory there named six requirements for a just war: just cause, right authority, right intention (that is, an intention in accord with the just cause), reasonable hope of success, proportionality (which he developed so as to include last resort), and noncombatant immunity, which he treated as a jus ad bellum requirement. In line with what has become the trademark of the American Catholic bishops on war, he opened this listing by reaffirming the idea of a presumption against war, which only satisfaction of these criteria could overcome. What shows clearly in his letter and the subsequent statement by the Conference of Catholic Bishops as a whole is the dominance of the presumption against war idea. Here, the requirements for providing a possible exception—a just use of military force—are stated so restrictively and prejudicially as to make them virtually impossible to meet. The presumption against war here has essentially turned into a rejection of war, that is, a functional pacifism.

## A BENCHMARK SECULAR VERSION OF THE JUST WAR IDEA

Among secular just war theorists involved in the recovery of just war thinking in American debate over armed force, Michael Walzer stands out. His 1977 book, *Just and Unjust Wars*, constitutes a benchmark every bit as important as Ramsey's work from the 1960s and the Catholic bishops' 1983 pastoral letter. While Walzer announced it as his intent to recover the just war idea for contemporary thinking about war, no more than Ramsey nor the Catholic bishops did he look back to the just war tradition for what it had to say or for guidance in how to understand the just war idea. So far as he looked to any historical models, they were to be found in international relations and international law. From these fields, he borrowed his terms for the jus ad bellum and the jus in bello: the "theory of aggression" and the "war convention." The content of each he developed by use of historical examples specifically chosen to express whatever point he was seeking to make about just war in terms of fundamental, human moral reactions to the experience of war. This was a powerful methodology, one that enabled the discussion and teaching of Walzer's conception of just war in secular contexts; his book has been for many years the principal just war text used in a basic course at the U.S. Military Academy, and in my own experience, anecdotal though it may be, it is the understanding of just war to which philosophers default. An unfortunate result is that those who get no further than Walzer's conception of just war have no conception of just war as a tradition of Western moral thought, a way of thinking that underlies the law of armed conflict in international law, nonrealist conceptions of the place of force in international relations, and many other things, quite apart from the specifically religious modern versions of just war. While he succeeds admirably in making the case that just war justifications and limits derive from fundamental human moral intuitions, my own judgment is that his reasoning needs to be accompanied by the disciplined criteria found in classic just war tradition.

As "to the content of Walzer's conception of just war, there is no presumption against war in Walzer's thought; rather, running throughout his work is the idea that force may work for good. But neither are there any of the classic or contemporary criteria stated as such in *Just and Unjust Wars*. To find these, one has to go to other sources, and Walzer himself has from time to time subsequently used the language of these criteria in his own writings.

Three elements in Walzer's analysis of war have provoked particular attention and are relevant for just war argumentation regarding the use of force against the Saddam Hussein regime. First, like Ramsey, Walzer was open to the use of military force for intervention in cases of grave humanitarian need. He hedged this about carefully, requiring that the need must be almost genocidal in character and noting that he had not been able to identify any cases of purely humanitarian motives in historical examples of military interventions. But the argument was made nonetheless, and in the context of debate over intervention in Somalia, Bosnia, Rwanda, and Kosovo during the 1990s, it tended to open the door to arguments for the use of military force to assist the victims of those conflicts. This same argument could have been used, but to my knowledge was not, in evaluation of President Bush's argument that the egregious violations of human rights perpetrated by the Saddam Hussein regime warranted use of military force to remove that regime.

While the argument for intervention bears on the question of the justification of resort to armed force, two other important elements in Walzer's thought bear on right conduct in the use of armed force. First, in his discussion of the rule of double effect, Walzer added a further restriction to the requirement that noncombatants not be directly, intentionally targeted: he held that this moral rule required soldiers to take steps, even at their own risk, to avoid collateral (indirect and formally unintentional) harm to noncombatants. This line of reasoning showed through in the arguments of various critics of the Kosovo bombing campaign, who carried it further to suggest that there is something immoral about bombing from high altitudes, where the air crews cannot be harmed by antiaircraft fire. Critics of the air campaign during Operation Iraqi Freedom used this same argument.

The second element in Walzer's thought on war, which has provoked particular attention, is his treatment of the idea of "supreme emergency." Developed in *Just and Unjust Wars* as part of a discussion of the British bombing of German cities during World War II, Walzer introduced this concept as a way of placing such bombing, which was intentionally directed at population centers, in the frame of just war reasoning. While utilitarians from the first have understood this to be an example of consequentialist moral reasoning—specifically, that the end justifies the means—I have always found a subtler and more morally profound argument here: that in the case of a genuine supreme emergency, when the very values of one's society and one's civilization are in danger of being overcome by a hostile foe, it is permissible to act in contravention of those values in order to seek to preserve them. Walzer thus notes that after the Nazi forces were defeated, Britain did not formally honor the officer who had ordered the bombing campaign, signifying disapproval of his methods. Whether the consequentialist interpretation of Walzer's reasoning or the one I have offered is accepted, there remains the basic moral question of whether it is ever justifiable to violate the norms of right conduct in war, and if it is, for what reasons, in what contexts, and for what duration. In the context of the war on terrorism, the supreme emergency argument bears on the question of whether it is ever justified to exceed established moral and legal limits in the treatment of prisoners and their interrogation. It also bears on whether there can be any justification for soldiers to violate the established norms of the law of armed conflict to gain military advantage against an otherwise superior force, as Iraqi fedayeen forces did during Operation Iraqi Freedom and as insurgents have subsequently done in opposing coalition forces and the new Iraqi government. Clearly, the supreme emergency idea—the idea that under certain extreme conditions, all restraints on the conduct of war may be ignored—is fundamentally threatening to the conception that basic moral restraints ought to be observed even in war. It also opens the door to war that is unrestrained not only on the side that determines itself to be threatened to the extreme but also on the other side, for behavior on one side will quickly be met by similar behavior on the other. The supreme emergency concept as Walzer first developed it was a nuanced and subtle attempt to fit a particular kind of military action—deliberate bombing of population centers—into some sort of moral framework. Generalized, though, it opens a can of very toxic worms: it becomes a rationale for warfare in which anything goes, whether toward noncombatants or toward combatants.

## THE CLASSIC JUST WAR IDEA REVISITED

The influence of all the above versions of recent just war thought are to be found in moral reflection on the use of military force in Iraq. I have criticized them all in presenting them, by noting their relation, or lack of relation, to the conception of just war as classically stated in the just war tradition. The just war idea is not free-floating, to be given whatever content one may think appropriate in whatever context. Understanding its meaning means engagement with the tradition out of which it comes and entering into dialog with the classical statement of the just war idea within that tradition. This is important to discipline just war thinking and keep it true to itself; however, it is also important because it is by engaging the historical tradition of just war that we get at the values that underlie it and the lasting concerns about human life in political community on which just war thinking is based and which it expresses.

I have been especially critical of the concept that the just war idea begins with a presumption against war or against the use of military force and that the function of the just war criteria is to override this general negative presumption. To think of the just war idea this way makes it over into something very different from what it properly is. I have outlined the particular contingent circumstances within which the presumption against war idea is based. Just war thinking in its classic form is based in something quite different—a conception of life in political community oriented to a just and peaceful order, in which the use of armed force is a necessary tool to be used by responsible political authority to protect that just and peaceful order in a world in which serious threats are not only possible but actual. In the presumption against war model, force itself is the moral problem, and peace is defined as the absence of the use of such force. In the just war model rightly understood, injustice and the threat of injustice are the fundamental moral problems, for in the absence of justice, the political community is not rightly ordered, and there is no real peace either in that community or in its relation to other political communities. Force here is not evil in itself; it takes its moral character from who uses it, from the reasons used to justify it, and from the intention with which it is used. These are, of course, the classic just war requirements of sovereign authority, just cause, and right intention, and they correspond directly to right order, justice, and peace, the goods at which political community should aim as defined in the Augustinian conception of politics within which just war tradition is soundly rooted. To be sure, force is evil when it is employed to attack the justice and peace of a political order oriented toward these goods, but it is precisely to defend against such evil that the use of force may be good. Just war tradition has to do with defining the possible good use of force, not finding exceptional cases when it is possible to use something inherently evil (force) for the purposes of good.

I have also criticized the priority given in some recent just war thinking to three moral criteria not found in classic statements of the just war idea. My concern with these is not simply that they are new, but that they are at best supportive concerns having to do with the wise practice of government, not primary concerns having to do with establishing and protecting the goods of politics themselves. To treat them as if they are of the same character as the requirements found in classic just war thought, or even as more important, warps just war reasoning. The traditional just war criteria—sovereign authority, just cause, and right intention, including the end of peace—are deontological in character; they impose duties on the person or people having ultimate moral responsibility for the good of the political community and for good relations among political communities. The newly added criteria—last resort, reasonable hope of success, and that the end result of the use of force be of more good than harm—are consequentialist in nature, requiring an estimate of outcomes and a weighing of the wisdom of resorting to force in a given case. These are clearly important concerns, and as I have said earlier, they are arguably concerns to which wise statecraft ought always to attend, although it is only within the last twenty years or so that they have regularly been included in listings of the requirements of just war jus ad bellum.

Once these consequentialist criteria are thus explicitly made part of jus ad bellum reasoning, the question is how to employ them. My view on this is summarized in figure 2.4. These recently introduced criteria are really different in character from the classic deontological criteria of traditional just war thought, and this needs to be recognized. Their function is secondary; they provide guidance as to when a particular use of force, already deemed justified by the primary criteria, is wise or unwise. Not everything that it is justified to do would be wise to do. Conversely, there may be actions that could be judged to satisfy the consequentialist criteria that would be patently unjust. Some things are wrong even though there may be good consequentialist reasons supporting them. The consequentialist criteria could be judged to be satisfied by directly and intentionally attacking noncombatants, for example, or by the torture of prisoners, or by an individual's undertaking the use of force for his or her own private reasons—however noble they might be claimed to be—and not out of responsibility for the good of the political community or the relations among political communities. But the consequentialist questions are not the first ones to be asked, as they have frequently been in recent just war thinking, and as we shall see in the debate over using force against Saddam Hussein and his regime.

Another issue with regard to the consequentialist criteria is who gets to make the call. The logic of the classic conception of just war places the judgment as to just cause and the duty to exercise right intention within the responsibility of the person or people in sovereign authority, and similarly the obligations to make judgments about wise statecraft required by the consequentialist criteria belong to those with ultimate responsibility for the public good. Moralists do not bear this responsibility, and moreover, as a class, moralists have no particular experience with the prudential exercise of statecraft. For a moralist to offer worst-case estimates (indeed, to offer any estimates at all, but in practice the ones offered have been worst-case estimates) of the extent of destruction to be expected from the use of force or of the likelihood of success, or to require that everything anyone can think of has been tried and has failed before the use of force can be moral is to abuse these consequentialist criteria in the worst possible way.

The purpose and proper function of the jus in bello criteria, those having to do with right conduct in the use of justified force, are quite different from those of the jus ad bellum, which has to do with determining whether resort to force is right in the first place. I have already noted that Ramsey's stress on the

**Figure 2.4   Using the Classic Just War Criteria Today**

**The jus ad bellum:** Criteria defining the right to resort to force.

**Deontological (primary) criteria:**

**Sovereign authority:**
The person or body authorizing the use of force must be the duly authorized representative of a sovereign political entity. The authorization to use force implies the ability to control and cease that use, that is, a well-constituted and efficient chain of command.
*Classic statement:* Reservation of the right to employ force to persons or communities with no political superior

**Just cause:**
The cause is the protection and preservation of value in the face of injustice.
*Classic Statement:* Defense of the common good, of the innocent against armed attack
Retaking persons, property, or other values wrongly taken
Punishment of evil

**Right intention:**
The intent must be in accord with the just cause and not territorial aggrandizement, intimidation, or coercion.
*Classic statement:* Negatively, evils to be avoided in war, including hatred of the enemy, "implacable animosity," "lust for vengeance," or desire to dominate. Positively, the aim of producing peace

**The aim of peace:**
The aim is the establishment of domestic and international stability, security, and peaceful interaction. It may include nation building, disarmament, or other measures to promote peace.
*Classic statement:* The positive aspect of the criterion of right intention

**Prudential (supportive) criteria:**

**Proportionality of ends:**
The overall good expected from the use of force must be greater than the harm expected. The levels and means of using force must be appropriate to the just ends sought. This criterion interacts with the other just as bellum criteria to determine the level, type, and duration of force applied.

**Last resort:**
Determination must be made at the time of the decision to employ force that no other means will achieve the justified ends sought. This criterion interacts with the other jus ad bellum criteria to determine the level, type, and duration of force applied.

**Reasonable hope of success:**
Prudential calculation must be made of the likelihood that the means used will produce the justified ends sought. This criterion interacts with the other jus ad bellum criteria to determine the level, type, and duration of force employed.

**The jus in bello:** Criteria defining right conduct in employing force

**Noncombatant protection/immunity:**
This criterion includes definition of noncombatancy, the requirement that noncombatants not be directly, intentionally targeted, and the requirement that other efforts to protect noncombatants in the way of combat be undertaken.
*Classic statement:* Lists of persons to be spared the harm of war (e.g., women, children, the aged, the infirm, and others deemed unable to wage war; also such groups as clergy, merchants, peasants on the land, and other people in activities not related to the prosecution of war)

**Proportionality of means:**
In a given tactical situation, the means employed should be proportionate to the task; also, means causing unnecessary or gratuitous harm are not to be used.
*Classic statement:* Attempts to limit weapons and the days allowed for fighting

requirements of right conduct in war has led to their being used as a way for those opposed to the use of force to argue against it. We will also see this same phenomenon in the arguments against using force to oust Saddam Hussein. For clarity's sake, surely it is morally important not to plan a use of force so as to include indiscriminate and disproportionate harm; rather, the aim should be to minimize both. But this is what the classic just war concept of right intention is about; the jus in bello restrictions are about how to behave in order to manifest such right intention. There is also an issue of honesty in the use of the jus in bello concerns to deny a jus ad bellum. Ramsey first identified this inversion of just war thinking in an essay included in his 1968 book responding to a pacifist who had used his thought in this way: Ramsey titled his response, "Can a Pacifist Tell a Just War?" His point was that the pacifist in question, James Douglass, had already made up his mind that all uses of armed force are morally wrong, so his use of just war terminology did not amount to an honest effort to follow just war reasoning where it might lead. One still finds this phenomenon, usually joined to an estimate of the destructiveness of the use of force as wildly indiscriminate and disproportionate, and we see it in the debate over using force to depose Saddam Hussein. It is a misuse of the just war idea.

Among right uses of the just war idea of right conduct in war, though, there are two somewhat different models of the relevant limits. One offered by Ramsey has been widely adopted in recent just war thinking: to define right conduct by two moral principles, discrimination and proportionality. The older model, that found in classic just war thought, is to define noncombatancy by lists of categories of people normally not involved in war (e.g., women, children, the aged and infirm, farmers on the land, merchants, travelers) and to limit the means of war by banning certain weapons or types of weapons deemed inherently indiscriminate or disproportionate in their effects. This model is preserved in the present-day law of armed conflicts: the 1949 Geneva Conventions (and their predecessors) define noncombatant immunity by naming classes of protected people, while the various treaties and other agreements seeking to limit or ban certain weapons (e.g., dumdum bullets and asphyxiating gases) or types of weapons (e.g., nuclear, biological, and chemical weapons) exemplify the contemporary version of the approach, which in the Middle Ages focused on trying to outlaw crossbows, bows and arrows, and siege weapons like the catapult. The 1977 Protocols to the 1949 Geneva Conventions introduced the ideas of discrimination (called "distinction" there) and proportionality as guides for decisions in matters not explicitly covered in the positive law, and this approach, in my judgment, is the best way to think of how to get the best from both of these models. The explicit lists of classes of non-combatants alone, and the specific bans or restrictions on particular weapons alone, do not cover every contingency; some guidance is needed for filling in the gaps in the positive requirements or extrapolating from them as new contingencies arise. At the same time, though, the principles of discrimination (or distinction) and proportionality by themselves require much reinventing of the wheel if they are used without reference to the settled consensus on who is a combatant and who a noncombatant and on what weapons or types of weapons may rightly be used in a just war. Sometimes, some very bad moral reasoning has resulted.

Some have argued, for example, that in modern war the principle of discrimination is meaningless since the structure of modern society is such that everyone is involved in his or her country's wars, and in any case, citizens may be assumed to favor their country's side, regardless of its justice or injustice. In response to the first line of argument, Ramsey found it necessary to remind readers that in any kind of war, at any time, some people are always noncombatants. He used the example of babies, but it does not take much extrapolation to add young children, the aged, and those rendered unable to fight by physical or mental illness. It does not take much more extrapolation to add all those classes of people listed in the classical just war listings. If some of these people are always noncombatants, and if others are normally to be assumed to be so, then it makes sense to say this up front. Of course, some people from classes normally assumed to be noncombatants may actually become directly involved in a combatant role in the conflict. But that is very different from saying that the combatant-noncombatant distinction is meaningless today.

As for the matter of personal sentiment, that question was addressed and answered centuries ago: this simply does not matter. The definition of combatancy and noncombatancy follows from direct involvement in prosecuting the war, not from one's citizenship or one's personal preference among the belligerents. It is action that matters, not attitude. For this reason, I regard the use of the term *civilian* in the Protocols to the Geneva Conventions as misleading: it is not civilian status that matters, as irregular soldiers may technically be civilians; what matters is whether people are engaged in combatant activity or not. The relevant moral term is *noncombatant*, even though the language of the protocols uses *civilian*, and this usage has seeped into the moral debate at times.

Bad moral reasoning has been much in evidence in the use of the principle of proportionality. One problem is that, as one finds it in recent debate, the jus ad bellum and jus in bello uses of this term are often not well distinguished. Another problem is that different contributors to the debate measure proportionality differently or not at all, simply declaring certain means "disproportionate." One claim, for example, is that the principle of proportionality, used in the in bello context, requires opposing force with similar force, as if armed conflict were a football game. This misunderstands what the principle of proportionality is about: determining when a particular use of force (a given weapon or tactic) is likely to produce more good than harm. In Operation Iraqi Freedom, for example, targeting for air strikes, in an effort to maximize the good results over the destruction caused, chose particular lines of attack over others, particular delivery systems—a Predator drone, say, as against a laser-guided bomb from an F-16 or a JDAM from far above, and the size and type of the weapon to be used in order to minimize overall destruction and collateral harm. This is the proper operational interpretation of the requirement of proportionality in international law, and moral usage would do well to follow its guide.

The concept of just war I have outlined here is the one I employ below as a tool for analyzing and critiquing the debate over using force to depose Saddam Hussein, the actual use of force in Operation Iraqi Freedom, and the lessons that should be learned from this debate and this conflict for future moral reflection on war. This is a conception that rests squarely on the classic statement of the just war idea found in just war tradition, but one that also seeks to take account of certain features that have become common in contemporary just war debate as a result of the way the recovery of just war thought has taken place over the last forty years. Readers who know my earlier work will recognize some evolution in the way I present the just war criteria—my current ranking the jus ad bellum criteria is the result of my study of the idea of sovereignty and its moral meaning over the last several years, as well as my going back to statements of the just war idea as offered by historical thinkers like Thomas Aquinas, Francisco de Vitoria, Martin Luther, and others. But the core of this conception has been there all along: that to think and speak seriously and with intellectual discipline about the idea of just war, one needs to take account of the historical just war tradition and engage the thinkers who shaped it in a continuing dialog. That is also my purpose in the analysis and critique offered in the following chapter.

# II

# THE WAR TO OUST SADDAM HUSSEIN: BEFORE

# 3

# THE DEBATE OVER USING FORCE AGAINST THE SADDAM HUSSEIN REGIME

## Was the Use of Force Justified?

### The Administration's Arguments

The moral debate over the use of military force against the Saddam Hussein regime in Iraq may be said to have begun in August 2002, with statements from Vice President Richard Cheney and Secretary of Defense Donald Rumsfeld arguing that Iraq's possession of chemical and biological weapons of mass destruction (WMD) and energetic effort to achieve nuclear-weapons capability might justify preemptive military action and the removal of the Saddam Hussein regime. This argument attracted a great deal of attention from the media, especially from critics of the war against Saddam Hussein's Iraq, and subsequent inspections and searches have revealed that, in fact, the regime's capacity for developing WMD was in tatters. But the regime had taken care to hide this and to suggest that it in fact possessed a robust WMD capability; thus, despite what is known now, in the debate of 2002–2003, there was general agreement among intelligence services in the West that Saddam Hussein's Iraq did possess significant chemical-weapons stocks, had a biological-weapons capability, and was intent on developing nuclear weapons as soon as possible. Vice President Cheney's and Secretary Rumsfeld's statements reflected that consensus. What was new in them was not the assessment of the

WMD threat posed by the Saddam Hussein regime but the opening of an argument for preemptive military action to remove his regime lest Iraq make such weapons available to terrorists for use against the United States. Although this argument opened the debate over using force against the Saddam Hussein regime, and although it has continued to be the focus of most attention and most controversy, this was not the only argument put forward for such action.

President Bush's September 12 speech to the U.N. General Assembly briefly echoed Vice President Cheney's and Secretary Rumsfeld's arguments in voicing the fear that Iraq's "outlaw regime" might supply terrorists with "the technologies to kill on a massive scale." But the burden of that speech was elsewhere; the president emphasized in detail the violations of the agreement that ended the Gulf War in 1991 and a host of Security Council resolutions stemming from Iraq's aggression against Kuwait and its behavior since the 1991 cease-fire, as well as Saddam Hussein's systematic and continuing oppression of the Iraqi people, his use of torture, assassination, and chemical warfare against his enemies, and his diversion of food-for-fuel money for his own purposes, while causing his people to suffer and die from lack of food and medical care. These were issues that others had been discussing in various contexts before the president's speech, but his raising of them there made them part of the administration's case for use of force against Iraq, thus solidified them as issues that ought to be addressed in the public debate. Subsequently, the president made these same three points in his State of the Union speech and in his brief address announcing the start of military action against the Saddam Hussein regime.

Put simply, these three public statements by President Bush put on the table three arguments for the justification of using U.S. military force against the Saddam Hussein regime. First was the argument for preemption: that use of such force is justified in order to preempt Hussein's using the chemical and biological weapons he now has and the nuclear weapons he is energetically seeking and close to having, possibly by making them available to terrorists. The second argument was for enforcement of international law: that use of military force is justified to enforce compliance with internationally agreed-on requirements adopted by the Security Council and imposed on Iraq after its 1990 aggression against Kuwait and to punish Iraq for the flouting of those requirements over the last decade. The third argument was to respond to egregious and continuing violations of human rights: that use of military force is justified to effect regime change, removing and punishing Saddam Hussein for his crimes against his own people and his neighbors, crimes that rise above the threshold of crimes against humanity, and replacing his regime with a better government, ideally one that is free, democratic, and committed to respecting human rights and promoting the common good. These were the arguments that needed to be examined with as much care as possible in the moral debate over the use of military force that took place during late 2002 and early 2003.

## EARLY EXAMPLES OF A JUST WAR
## CRITIQUE: NO TO PREEMPTION

Just war thinking has become an important element in American moral reflection on the use of military force, and so it was in the debate over the use of force against the Saddam Hussein regime. While neither President Bush nor spokespeople for his administration employed just war language explicitly (as President George H. W. Bush had done in 1990, prior to the use of military force to roll back Iraq's aggression against Kuwait), use of just war language and ideas figured prominently in the responses, both supportive and critical, to their arguments. In this chapter, I examine several prominent examples of such responses, focusing on two factors: how far the responses actually engaged the three justifying causes identified by President Bush and how well the responses understood and applied the criteria of just war to which they appealed.

The moral debate of 2002–2003, unfortunately, did not get very far in grappling with the three justifying causes named by President Bush for use of force against the Saddam Hussein regime. Just as in the summer of 2002, the administration's case for using military force seemed to boil down to this line of thinking, so the moral critics of such action responded by zeroing in on preemption to the exclusion of the other issues. Two early examples show how this response developed. First, in mid-September, Bishop Wilton D. Gregory, president of the U.S. Conference of Catholic Bishops, took exactly this limited line against preemption in a letter to President Bush arguing against any use of military force. Second, later that month a statement signed by one hundred Christian ethicists was issued opposing any preemptive use of force. Not only did these two statements wrongly focus on preemption to the exclusion of the other justifying reasons that had by then been offered, but their moral analysis was also flawed in other ways, as we shall presently see.

We turn first to the Gregory letter, which began by referencing the American bishops' trademark idea, that of a moral presumption against the use of armed force, an idea that is unique to them and never appeared in Catholic doctrine on war—or the broader just war tradition—prior to the American bishops' pastoral letter *The Challenge of Peace* in 1983. Then, Bishop Gregory provided a list of the just war requirements, which he identified as just cause, right authority, right intention, reasonable hope of success, proportionality, and noncombatant immunity. These are all important concerns, but notably missing was the aim of achieving a justly ordered peace, a core element of just war tradition from its beginnings. But on further reading in this letter, one may wonder whether anything could ever satisfy the bishop's concerns as stated there. In the first place, the presumption against force idea implies that force is inherently morally suspect rather than (as just war tradition rightly understood has always held) a possible tool for good or evil, depending on the user, the justification, the intention, and other circumstances. The various just war criteria, according to this reasoning, exist only to provide exceptions, to override this general presumption. The use of force is, thus, generally a bad thing. The idea that it can in some cases produce positive good has been discarded; force as such is always morally problematic, and when it is used, it does not lose that problematic character. (This may suggest why Bishop Gregory, speaking for the U.S. Conference of Catholic Bishops, did not include the aim of peace in his listing of the criteria for a just war: if the use of force is itself morally problematic, even when just, how can it aim at peace?) So, when Bishop Gregory applied the just war criteria that he listed to the case of a possible use of force against the Saddam Hussein regime, he approached the question not by asking whether there is an evil that just use of force may possibly right but by postulating that the use of force is itself an evil that must be avoided if possible. That skews the moral argument and moves it decisively away from the approach taken in the just war tradition proper.

As to the just war criteria themselves as named by Bishop Gregory, he cast his treatment of the requirement of just cause entirely in terms of the argument over preemption. Now, the justification of preemption is inherently difficult to demonstrate publicly because doing so before the fact may compromise intelligence gathering and cost lives. Thus, not surprisingly, the Gregory letter found that the argument for preemption did not satisfy the requirement of just cause. Although this letter was issued shortly after the president's U.N. speech, it made no mention of the other lines of argument for just cause laid out there. (Nor did a subsequent statement of the entire Conference of Catholic Bishops, based on the Gregory letter.) Under the rubric of the requirement of right authority, Bishop Gregory called for congressional authorization, broad public consensus, and international authorization. Since all of these requirements were already well on the way toward existing at the time of this letter and since they were later met, iterating these moral requirements did nothing to support the opposition to the use of force expressed in Bishop Gregory's letter. Indeed, they carried the opposite implication. But it is a different story with regard to the remaining requirements listed in the letter and the use made of them by Bishop Gregory: reasonable hope of success, proportionality of good achieved over harm done, and observance of noncombatant immunity. Commenting on these criteria, the letter painted a worst-case scenario in which the use of force against Iraq would cause regional instability, have a severe impact on the Iraqi population, escalate into a wider conflict, violate the immunity of noncombatants, and have other unpredictable bad consequences. These arguments echoed judgments put forward by spokesmen for the National Conference of Catholic Bishops in 1990–1991, which painted a similar scenario to call into question the justification for use of armed force against Iraq to restore Kuwait after Iraq had aggressively attacked and annexed that country. Bishop Gregory's argument as stated seems intended to reinforce the presumption against the use of force, not to leave open the possibility that resort to force might be justified in this case. Employing the prudential criteria as he did makes just war argument into a form of utilitarian consequentialism, not the obligation-based moral logic that it properly is. I have already described what I hold to be the right understanding of the just war idea and its use in moral analysis, and I will have more to say about this below. I disagree significantly with some elements in the conception of just war employed by the U.S. Catholic bishops. This tendency toward utilitarianism is one such difference. In any case, in the specific context of the Gregory letter, one may reasonably wonder what special wisdom the president of the U.S. Catholic Conference brings to making a prudential judgment on the effects of a military action against the Saddam Hussein regime. This kind of judgment belongs properly to those entrusted with the office of government, and moral analysis oversteps its role when it tries to usurp that judgment for itself.

What we see in Bishop Gregory's argument is an expression of a wider phenomenon. For most of the last forty years, American and Western European just war thought has focused on the particular problems of nuclear weapons and the experience of the American involvement in Vietnam. Thinking about war in terms of an expected nuclear holocaust and in terms of rejection of the type of war represented by the Vietnam conflict led some to what the late theologian and just war theorist Paul Ramsey called a *bellum contra bellum justum*, a war against just war, a position others have described as "just war pacifism" or "modern war pacifism." This position essentially holds that given the destructive capabilities of modern warfare, a just war is now impossible. The U.S. Catholic bishops' presumption against war is part of the legacy of this broader moral unease with the idea that contemporary warfare can be just. As the bishops have developed and applied it in various contexts since 1983, they have transformed the traditional just war categories from moral concerns to guide the practice of statecraft into a series of moral obstacles that, as described and interpreted, are arguments against the use of moral force's ever being justifiable. The regular advancing of worst-case scenarios as unbiased moral advice underscores the opposition to uses of armed force as such and distorts the application of just war reasoning. The result is a functional pacifism, despite the claim that this is what the just war idea requires. The Gregory letter, exemplifying this, surely goes far in advising prudential caution, but it succeeds rather less well as a useful source of moral analysis regarding the use of military force against the Saddam Hussein regime.

The statement of the one hundred Christian ethicists was only one sentence long, and its exclusive focus was to reject preemption: "As Christian ethicists, we share a common moral presumption against a pre-emptive war on Iraq by the United States." But one may wonder what is added to a public statement against preemption by a group of American citizens when they explicitly identify themselves as "Christian ethicists." This statement was a political act, not a case of moral analysis. The signers spoke as private individuals since the study of Christian ethics, a broad field, should not be taken to imply that they have any special expertise in the ethics of war or government. Some of those who signed this statement, including Stanley Hauerwas of Duke University Divinity School, one of the principal sponsors, Duane Friesen of Bethel College, and Glen Stassen of Fuller Theological Seminary, are pacifists, opposed to all uses of military force. It is not exceptional that they should sign a statement opposing preemptive use of force in this instance. They would presumably be against any prospective use of military force for whatever reason, whether preemptive or not. Others, though, thought of themselves as using just war reasoning and understood the statement as stating a conclusion implied by such reasoning. Thus, the second of the statement's principals, Shaun Casey of Wesley Theological Seminary, identified himself to the press as a just war ethicist and estimated that "the majority [of the signatories] are just-war," going on to describe this position in terms of the idea that just war theory begins with a presumption against the use of force and then spells out "permissible exceptions." This statement, then, so far as its reflection of just war thinking is concerned, employed a version of just war theory similar to that used by Bishop Gregory. But unlike the Gregory letter, the statement offered only a conclusion, without any supporting reasoning. One might have wished for an articulation of the differences among the signatories on the content and meaning of the just war idea and whether it matters at all that the pacifists, opposed to any use of force for whatever reason at any time, focused on preemptive use of force in this instance. As for the nonpacifists among the signers of this statement, one might have wished to hear their reasons for opposing preemptive use of force, as well as an indication of whether other possible justifications might lead them to different conclusions and to what extent consideration of the other just war criteria might be relevant in considering this case. Or is the presumption against war here so strong that under no reasonably foreseeable circumstances could there be an exception to it? If so, then the version of just war thinking used here is no more than another example of a functional pacifism. None of this was provided in the statement, which was a simple rejection of preemptive use of armed force against Iraq on the basis of a presumption against war claimed in common by the pacifists and the nonpacifists who signed the statement. Whatever its effect on the political argument, this statement was worth very little as a contribution to the public moral debate.

## PROBLEMS WITH THE FOCUS ON PREEMPTION

I have highlighted these two early entries into the moral debate over whether the use of force against the Saddam Hussein regime was justified because I want to draw attention to the focus in them, as in much of the public debate since, on preemption and to suggest that this focus has been misguided.

In the terms of moral analysis, the problem with an argument for preemption is centrally this: preemption is not inherently wrong or right, but it is extremely difficult to justify. For it to be justified, there must be a clear and present danger. While the administration and others favorable to the use of military force against Saddam Hussein's regime made a powerful case as to the danger itself, they did not demonstrate clearly, even with Secretary of State Colin Powell's forceful U.N. presentation, that the danger was present, in the sense of an attack definitely intended and in the process of preparation. We now know that the danger was not present, but again, the debate was about the prospect, and that is where moral decision making has to take place. That the danger is present, as I suggested earlier, is hard to demonstrate in cases like this because the necessary knowledge may be available only through sensitive intelligence sources.

The administration offered one very suggestive new consideration on the matter of what counts as preemption. The idea that preemption is sometimes justified is far from new: Hugo Grotius, writing in the seventeenth century, recognized that the preemptive use of force can sometimes be justified (although he did not use the term *preemption*; this is present-day usage), but he cautioned against allowing "any sort of fear" as the necessary justification. His own example of a convincing test was "if my assailant seizes a weapon with an obvious intent of killing me." A later version of this test was the massing of an army on one's borders, and by the beginning of the twentieth century, the accepted test was the mobilization of an enemy's forces, the necessary first step toward war. But the test has continued to evolve. The Israeli air strike against Egyptian and Syrian air power in the 1967 Middle East war was roundly criticized by those who applied the older tests, but in the aftermath of that strike, a consensus seems to have formed that preparation for invasion can be signaled not only by the massing of land troops but also by the clear preparation for an air strike, coupled with the manifest intent to attack. The Bush administration added to the debate the proposition that, coupled with evidence of intent, the existence of WMD in the hands of an enemy serves to justify preemptive use of force. Had there in fact been such weapons, I believe this would have become a new standard test of when preemption is justified. That Saddam Hussein's Iraq did not in fact have such weapons does not dispose of the argument. Is the concrete effort to obtain such weapons itself evidence of malicious intent that justifies use of force to cancel out that effort? This is a question that remains vital, especially when one thinks of cases like North Korea and Iran.

As to the right role of the moralist in the debate over preemption, a moralist working within the just war tradition may make clear that there must be justification, but it is going beyond this role to pass judgment on the facts of the case so that preemption is presented as morally impossible. The role of making such a judgment does not belong to the moralist but is among the obligations of those holding the office of government, or to put it in terms of the just war tradition, it is the responsibility of the person or people in sovereign authority. By just war reasoning properly understood, the requirement that there be such authority for the use of force gives to the person or people holding such authority the right and the obligation to make the determination of justification; people not in that position of authority may give their opinions, and they may participate in holding their political leaders to account for their decisions and actions, but they do not have the right to decide whether preemption is justified on their own.

Moral discussion of the question of preemption is complicated—and, I think, distorted—by the assumptions of the Westphalian system of international order as incorporated in positive international law, where there is a tendency to regard first use of force across a national border as always wrong and second use as always justified. This version of the aggressor-defender distinction does not well fit the case of threats that, if carried through, have the capacity to annihilate a significant part of the population of a state or even, in the case of a relatively small state, to wipe it out entirely. In other words, the status of international law regarding the use of force does not well fit the problems posed by WMD or the consideration of preemption as a means of dealing with such a threat that is deemed credible. I say this not to suggest how we should come out in rethinking this matter, for it is a very complicated one, but only to emphasize that the proliferation of WMD imposes a great need to reconsider it. It is likely, I think, that there is no one-case-fits-all solution, just as the old aggressor-defender construct has not provided such a solution in practice. In the meantime, the state of positive international law aids potential attackers, and moral consideration of preemption should proceed independently of the first-use, second-use distinction. For my part, I have gradually moved to the position that there is a serious case for preemption when an avowed enemy has WMD, and all other means of dealing with this threat offer no hope of removing it. But I think there is no moral consensus on this. That is another way of saying what I have already said differently: that given the lack of agreement on clear guidelines for thinking about preemption, it is wrong to focus so exclusively on the question of preemption when thinking about the justification of using armed force against Saddam Hussein.

## BROADENING THE JUST WAR CRITIQUE

A third prominent statement from the fall of 2002, one explicitly employing just war language and referring it directly to President Bush's U.N. speech, was a letter dated October 3, initiated by Richard D. Land, president of the Ethics and Religious Liberty Commission of the Southern Baptist Convention and cosigned by four other leading evangelicals. In contrast to the letter of Bishop Gregory and the statement of the one hundred Christian ethicists, the Land letter did not mention preemption at all. Although it referred to the aim of disarming "Saddam Hussein and his weapons of mass destruction" as "a just cause," it described this entirely in terms of defense, citing Hussein's past actions ("he has attacked his neighbors, used weapons of mass destruction against his own people, and harbored terrorists from the Al Qaeda terrorist network") proving him to be a threat, and concluded its discussion of just cause with the statement, "Disarming and neutralizing Saddam Hussein is to defend freedom and freedom-loving people from state-sponsored terror and death." The Land letter thus rolled together the three justifying causes laid out by the president, recasting all of them in terms of the idea of defense.

Like the Gregory letter, the Land letter continued by providing a list of just war criteria and testing the prospective use of force against them. Unlike Gregory, however, Land and his colleagues concluded that the tests had been satisfied, leaving the choice to employ force up to the president. The just war criteria as named in this letter began with just cause and continued with the requirements of just intent, identified as "liberty for the Iraqi people"; last resort, satisfied by Saddam Hussein's repeated breaking of the Security Council resolutions and other agreements; "authorization by legitimate authority," identified as "the government of the United States"; limited goals and a reasonable expectation of success, described as met by the president's stated policies; noncombatant immunity, identified as the intention not to target civilians and to minimize noncombatant casualties; and last, proportionality, described as satisfied in these terms: "We believe that the cost of not dealing with this threat now will only succeed in greatly increasing the cost in human lives and suffering" that will result from the need to confront Saddam Hussein "in the not too distant future." That this list differs from Bishop Gregory's in significant respects is clear: both the specific moral requirements named and the order in which they are listed are different, and as noted earlier, the Land letter concluded that these requirements were satisfied, in sharp contrast to the arguments advanced in the Gregory letter. It is of special importance that the Land letter did not characterize the just war idea as beginning with a presumption against war. Rather, if anything, its tone throughout suggested that, in this particular case, the just war criteria pointed toward the use of armed force as the only way to meet the threat posed by Saddam Hussein and to punish him and his regime for past evildoing.

## THE ARGUMENT FROM INTERNATIONAL LAW

Although the Land letter effectively collapsed all three of President Bush's justifying causes into its own argument for defense, no more than the Gregory letter or the statement of the one hundred Christian ethicists did it directly address the second and third justifying reasons laid out by the president. Let us now take a closer look at these.

The second argument for the use of force against the Saddam Hussein regime put forward in the U.N. speech and later was that the use of force was justified to enforce compliance and punish noncompliance with existing agreements, resolutions, and international law. The moral dimensions of this argument were all but lost in the international debate during late 2002 and early 2003 over whether yet another Security Council resolution (or perhaps more) might be needed and how far to try yet one more round of international arms inspections. Arguments over these issues were effectively political in nature, but they obscured the deeper question of whether, in moral and legal terms, the behavior of Iraq under Saddam Hussein over the past twelve years deserved, at last, a robust military response. But there were entries into the debate that recognized the moral force of this justification in terms of international law. An important example was a statement from mid-November 2002 composed under the auspices of the Institute for American Values, which had earlier issued the widely circulated justification for the war on terror, "What We're Fighting For" (a statement to which I was a signatory), which took this as a convincing rationale justifying "at least preparing to attack Iraq" (3):

> The U.N. Security Council resolutions on disarmament and weapons inspections in Iraq, passed in 1991, have been flagrantly, and so far with impunity, violated by the Iraqi regime. The U.S. and its allies should have been willing to fight a just war over this issue years ago, especially when Iraq effectively expelled the U.N. weapons inspectors in 1998.

This is also a point that pundits like Tom Friedman and Bill Keller made forcefully in their own contributions to the developing public debate. As Keller put it in a *New York Times* op-ed article on February 22,

> A little time in the archives is a reminder that this [likely upcoming] war is in many respects a continuation of [the 1990–1991 Gulf War]. We are calling to account a tyrant who has flouted the terms of his surrender. It's not just that we have been here before; technically, we never left. (A 17)

For me, this line of reasoning offered the most straightforward justification, in terms of international law, for the use of military force against the Saddam Hussein regime. This justification was there from the beginning, or rather since the first violation of the 1991 truce. It has long been a principle of customary international law that breaking a truce reopens hostilities at the point just before the truce; in this case, given the repeated and egregious violations of the terms of the truce, this principle justified the removal of the Saddam Hussein regime that was not undertaken in 1991. Because the ultimate justification of this argument reached back to the obligation to respond to the 1990 invasion of Kuwait, it also fit closely the conditions of the traditional just war idea of just cause.

Although not included in contemporary conventional listings of the just war criteria, the historical just war tradition took the obligations incurred in truces with deep seriousness. Deliberate entry into a truce with intent to break its terms was understood as an act of deception inherently opposed to the aim of establishing a just and peaceful postwar order, which, in the end, is what the just use of force is all about. In terms of the law of war, deliberate breaking of the terms of a truce reopened the conflict again at the point at which the truce was made and gave the belligerent who was wronged the rights he had up to the point when the truce was signed. We may recall the argument of 1991, after Operation Desert Storm, over whether the coalition forces should have moved on to occupy Baghdad and depose the Saddam Hussein regime. Raising this same question in 2002–2003 was not to introduce a new matter, on the reasoning just summarized: the deliberate and repeated violation of the 1991 truce by Saddam Hussein's regime in principle reopened the Gulf War of 1990–1991 and justified resumed military action against the regime itself. Whether it would be prudential to do so—the focus of the Catholic bishops' and other objections—was another matter entirely, but the question of justification for using military force against the regime that had so flagrantly and repeatedly violated the 1991 truce, in my reading, was not at all doubtful in light of reasoning based in the historical just war tradition.

## THE HUMAN RIGHTS ARGUMENT

Now, let me turn to the third argument, that Saddam Hussein and his regime deserved to be deposed and replaced because of their evil behavior. Again, President Bush used this argument to justify resort to force, but in the public debate, it was columnists like Friedman and Keller who advanced this argument most forcefully, and it was notably absent among those from the religious sector who only a few years earlier had used this line of reasoning to justify the use of military force in places like Rwanda, Bosnia, and Kosovo. This human rights–based argument is especially interesting and rich morally in its full range. Given the strong moral support that emerged in the 1990s for the idea that military intervention is justified in cases of gross abuses of human rights, there was a clear opening for a moral debate in 2002 that, following the indictment first voiced by President Bush in his U.N. speech, held Saddam Hussein to account for his well-attested-to history of torture, murder, and cruel oppression—that is, a moral debate that treated Saddam Hussein like Slobodan Milošević or the leaders of the Rwandan genocide. I have spoken earlier of the problems I find in the reasoning of the U.S. Catholic bishops on the use of military force. In 1993, though, they issued a statement (*The Harvest of Justice*) in which they declared humanitarian intervention a duty in cases of gross human rights violations, observed that claims of sovereignty by those engaged in such violations have no absolute status in Catholic teaching, and accepted use of force as a form that intervention might take. Other religious bodies and many other moralists, Christian ethicists and otherwise, accepted the same basic argument, favoring the use of intervention up to and including the use of military force to stop violations and punish violators. But such voices were not heard in the debate over using force against Saddam Hussein. Were the rights of Iraqis less important than those of Bosnians, Kosovars, and Rwandans? Or did the fact that the United States had national-interest reasons for moving against Saddam Hussein mean that any use of force in this case would be immoral, as a 1998 resolution of the U.S. Presbyterian Church formulated the right of intervention? Again, the moral debate of the fall and winter of 2002–2003 failed in not addressing this dimension of the question of whether to use force to depose Saddam Hussein and his regime. The later debate, right up to the initiation of Operation Iraqi Freedom, also failed to do so.

## LATER EXAMPLES OF JUST WAR ARGUMENT

In the later stages of the moral debate, an important shift took place away from the question of preemption and toward whether the use of force in this case was a last resort. The criterion of last resort, as I noted in chapter 3, is a relatively recent addition to the just war requirements for moral resort to force. Whereas the older criteria, sovereign authority, just cause, and right intention, including the aim of establishing peace, establish duties or obligations for the person or people in sovereign authority, the criterion of last resort and its associated criteria, equally recent, of reasonable hope of success and overall proportionality of good over harm establish prudential tests, requiring that a judgment be made as to the consequences both of resorting to force and of not resorting to force. The classic criteria tell when a use of armed force is just; the newer criteria have to do with whether, even if it is known to be just, a use of armed force is likely be unwise. The prudential criteria are thus secondary to and supportive of the classic ones, which remain primary for the moral consideration of the question of whether to employ force.

Often in recent just war reasoning, though, the criterion of last resort has been presented as if it were the first or second thing to think about. Also, very often this criterion is presented as it was by the U.S. Catholic bishops in their influential *The Challenge of Peace*: "For resort to war to be justified, all peaceful alternatives must have been exhausted" (Paragraph 96). Stated in this way, the criterion of last resort is effectively impossible to satisfy, for it is always possible to introduce yet another "peaceful alternative," however difficult or unlikely its achievement may be. The language may be that of just war, but the result is pacifist, always ruling out resort to force. For the last-resort requirement to be meaningful as a guide to prudence in political decisions, it has to have a different meaning: that a broad range of nonmilitary alternatives must be carefully thought through, and any genuinely promising ones must have been tried and failed to produce the desired result (which, it will be recalled, for just war tradition means achieving a justly ordered peace).

Two op-ed pieces that appeared within two days of each other on March 7 and 9, 2003, in the *New York Times* illustrate right and wrong uses of the criterion of last resort in the debate over whether to use force against Saddam Hussein's Iraq. One, "What a Little War in Iraq Could Do," was by Michael Walzer; the other, "Just War—Or a Just War?" was by former U.S. president Jimmy Carter.

Walzer, in fact, addressed both wrong and right uses of the idea of last resort. Noting that when the French spoke of the use of force as a "last resort," they were denying that force was already in use against Saddam Hussein's Iraq—what Walzer called the "little war"—although they were "not participating in it in any significant way." Indeed, he went on, "the opponents of the big war have not been prepared to join or support or even acknowledge the work that the little war requires." They, like other opponents of the war, offered no "plausible alternative"—only that there must be no resort to force. This, as Walzer saw well, illustrates use of the last-resort criterion as a way of avoiding use of force entirely.

Walzer's own way was to define a plausible alternative, several specific steps to intensify the little war that was already under way: to extend the northern and southern no-fly zones, to impose "smart sanctions," and "to challenge the French to make good on their claim that force is indeed a last resort by mobilizing troops of their own and sending them to the Gulf." Would taking these steps have prevented the "big war," the launching of the offensive to depose Saddam Hussein and his regime and to remake Iraq? We will never know. But the important thing in the present context is that Walzer took care to define his own concept of last resort by a genuinely "plausible alternative," not an alternative entirely devoid of any use of force, to be sure, but one that built on the limited uses of force already being applied.

President Carter, early in his article, pronounced himself "thoroughly familiar with the principles of a just war"; he continued by listing those principles as follows: "The war must be waged only as a last resort, with all nonviolent options exhausted"; "The war's weapons must discriminate between combatants and noncombatants"; "Its violence must be proportional to the injury we have suffered"; "The attackers must have legitimate authority sanctioned by the society they profess to represent"; and "The peace it establishes must be a clear improvement over what exists." President Carter's listing put the criterion of last resort first, as if it were the most important, and defined it in the most restrictive way: all nonviolent options must first have been exhausted before resort to force can be justified. He did not offer any specific alternatives, and as noted earlier, this way of defining the last-resort criterion is effectively open-ended; there is no end to the possible alternatives that must be tried and exhausted, provided they are nonviolent.

But more broadly, President Carter's version of just war disordered the just war principles, left out some of the most important, and stated those named in ways not consonant with their meaning in just war tradition. First, as to its disorder, President Carter's listing jumbled the criteria having to do with the question of whether force is justified and of how to use force after it has been deemed justified. The only two *jus ad bellum* ideas that are part of the deontological core of the tradition, the requirements of sovereign authority and the end of peace, came last when they are of first importance by the standards of the tradition. As for the criterion of last resort, putting this prudential criterion in first place gave it a priority it does not have in classic just war thinking and a prominence it does not deserve. The same goes for putting the prudential criterion of proportionality third. As I noted earlier, these prudential tests are relatively new to just war thinking, dating back only to the last forty years, and in terms of the logic of the just war idea, they have to do with the wisdom of doing what has already been determined to be justified. That is, they are about whether it is worth the risk to do what we know is right. This is a question that should be asked, but it is not the first or most important question to ask.

Among the questions not asked in President Carter's listing of the just war requirements was whether there was just cause for the use of force against the Saddam Hussein regime and whether the intention of overthrowing him was in accord with that cause. The article said nothing at all about these fundamental matters.

Finally, the article stated and explained the just war requirements in ways that distorted their meaning. Last resort, as already argued, does not require that "all nonviolent options [be] exhausted" but that among the alternatives reasonably judged to respond adequately to the threat, to embody right intention, and to hold out a hope of establishing a justly ordered peace, resort to force should be last. It has to do with identifying and judging among promising alternatives, not with an indefinite effort to try to exhaust every nonviolent option that anyone may identify. President Carter's way of thinking about last resort here participated in the same fallacy as Bishop Gregory's: dependence on a worst-case scenario of what use of force means. Carter wrote:

> The first stage of our widely publicized war plan is to launch 3,000 bombs and missiles on a relatively defenseless Iraqi population within the first few hours of an invasion, with the purpose of so damaging and demoralizing the people that they will change their obnoxious leader.

That is, the use of force is about intense and highly destructive attacks on the noncombatant population to get them to change their government. So much for the aim of discriminating between combatants and noncombatants; war aims at noncombatants. President Carter's language described the aim of strategic bombing as originally defined by its proponents, but it did not describe what just war is about. Nor, as a matter of fact, did it match what the U.S. administration and military leaders insisted to be the aim of the "shock and awe" campaign: to damage and demoralize the Saddam Hussein regime, to destroy its ability to function, and to overthrow it by military action. Those are aims consistent with the just war idea. It is important to recognize this and to hold the use of force to these aims.

On proportionality, many competing meanings have been offered since this idea first began to be used in discussions of the just use of force. If one focuses only on punishment for wrong already done, then President Carter's language fits. But if one is thinking instead of the aim of restoring a justly ordered peace, the right meaning of this criterion is to measure the good achieved against two measures of harm: that which will likely be done if force is not used, and that which the force itself creates. This is what we find, for example, in the Land letter discussed earlier.

As to the matter of authority, President Carter's article described the requirement as sanction "by the society they profess to represent"; this would seem to have been satisfied by congressional support and the polls, although it is important to remember that the traditional moral language has to do with the exercise of sovereign responsibility to ensure the society's good and to protect it against threats to that good. In any case, it is curious that after this initial definition relating to approval from American society, the paragraph in question had entirely to do with arguing that there is no international sanction or "international authority." Whether this is so is a proper subject for debate (Carter himself offered that "the unanimous vote of approval in the Security Council to eliminate Iraq's weapons of mass destruction can still be honored"), but in just war terms, sovereign authority to use force is a property of a given political community, and that imposes various conditions on it. Amid the talk of the need for U.N. authorization, it is worth noting that the United Nations itself lacks several important attributes of sovereign authority: it is not in fact sovereign but takes its power from the agreement of its constituent states; it is not responsible to the people of the world but only to these states; it lacks command-and-control capabilities, thus cannot direct the use of force responsibly; and in the end, it cannot be held accountable for its actions the way an individual state or its government can be. Security Council approval is important as a statement of consensus, but the lack of that consensus does not take away the right of individual states to act according to their reading of their responsibilities.

Finally, as to the aim of peace, the Carter article was correct as far as it went—"The peace it establishes must be a clear improvement over what exists"—but it did not go far enough. The classic just war idea of the aim of peace is to aim at establishing a social order that embodies justice and, because of this, is at peace within itself and with other societies. This is a great deal more than improving on what exists, although such improvement is a step on the way, and to achieve it is to accomplish good. President Carter's argument was that the use of force is likely to end up having the opposite result. Again, that is a fair argument, but it is one over which there is serious disagreement. Not to be challenged, though, is the the aim of achieving peace and not increasing injustice, chaos, and war.

The just war tradition is deeply embedded in Western culture, and I believe it continues to have fundamental implications for how we ought to think about political responsibility and how it should function in the world. But this means working with the tradition on its own terms. It is good to invoke the idea of just war as part of the moral debate over the use of force against the Saddam Hussein regime, but simply using some of the terms of the just war idea and filling them with one's own content does not do the idea justice.

## IMPORTANT BUT NEGLECTED ISSUES IN
## THE JUST WAR DEBATE

Let me turn to two particular issues raised within just war tradition that deserved fuller reflection in the 2002–2003 debate.

First, the question of sovereignty is critical. The position on the rights of sovereignty taken by the Catholic bishops in their 1993 statement fit well with the classic just war idea of sovereignty. As stated there, the rights of sovereignty are not absolute; the protections of sovereignty do not extend to those rulers guilty of serious violations of the rights of their people or others. By contrast with the conception of sovereignty implied in Bishop Gregory's 2002 treatment of the authority necessary for just war, the 1993 statement reflects the classic Christian understanding of the sources, obligations, and limits of political authority by which the rights of sovereignty are linked to its obligations. Historically, this is a position common to both Catholic tradition and Reformation Protestantism: Luther, Calvin, and the other Reformers took essentially this same position. This same idea of sovereignty characterized Western political philosophy as late as the American and French revolutions but has been replaced in more recent international law and practice by what is commonly referred to today as the "Westphalian system." Under the older idea, sovereignty was an essentially moral construct; a person (or people) in sovereign authority is responsible for the good of his, her, or their political community, for the "common weal." This implied establishing an order that served justice and achieved peace. Also implied as a part of this responsibility was an obligation to other political communities to support order, justice, and peace in and among them. Failure to discharge the sovereign's obligations removed the rights of sovereignty. This line of reasoning is found, in different ways, in both the Declaration of Independence and the French Declaration of the Rights of Man. In contrast with this essentially moral conception of sovereignty is that regularly associated with the Peace of Westphalia and embodied in the U.N. system, whereby sovereignty is defined by recognized governmental control over a particular territory and its inhabitants. This conception may be read to allow any government total immunity from interference in the way it handles its internal affairs and the way it treats its people. Thus, Slobodan Milošević, on his first appearance before the International Tribunal for the Former Yugoslavia, denied the authority of that court to indict and try him, claiming sovereign immunity because he was head of state when the acts in question occurred. Similarly, Saddam Hussein justified his resistance to weapons inspections, as well as other resolutions adopted after the 1990–1991 war to punish and constrain Iraq, by claiming they infringed on Iraq's sovereignty. According to the older, moral understanding of sovereignty, though, he forfeited the right to sovereign immunity and, indeed, the right to govern Iraq with his tyrannical exercise of government. In this conception, his crimes meant he could rightly be deposed and replaced with a leader who served the proper ends of political authority.

This idea, with its implications, has been seen at work in the indictments handed down by the International Tribunal for the Former Yugoslavia and that for Rwanda. Indeed, although the idea of war-crimes tribunals for deposed tyrants and their regimes is relatively new, that of removing and replacing an evil regime is not new at all in international politics: consider relatively recent examples such as Tanzania's deposing of Idi Amin in Uganda, Vietnam's deposing of Pol Pot and the Khmer Rouge in Cambodia, and the United States' removal of Manuel Noriega in Panama. Regime change, where the regime in question is guilty of cruel and tyrannical oppression or some other form of gross criminality, is not an innovation; it is a feature of the international order. Rather than there being a duty not to seek to effect regime change in such cases, which is the implication of the rights of sovereignty according to the Westphalian system, there may in fact be a duty to do so, both on behalf of the immediate victims of a regime's cruelty and on behalf of the international order itself.

The traditional just war idea of just cause allows the use of force to punish evil, and this surely applied in the case of Saddam Hussein and his regime. Indeed, this point was made, as noted earlier, in the Land letter's discussion of just cause for the use of force, although not in the other examples of just war reasoning we have examined. But another of the core just war concepts, which must always be honored, is that the aim of such force must include the establishment of peace. Here, a further dimension of this line of argument emerges: one is obligated, if one uses force to remove an evildoer from power, to replace his government with one that exercises sovereign authority for good, not evil, and that can create an order that serves justice and peace. Thus, regime change means not only getting rid of Hussein but creating a democratic Iraq that can serve as a model for the region, an idea put forward by the Bush administration and taken up pundit Thomas Friedman among others. This is a very important idea, and one that deserved serious attention within the moral debate. In retrospect, the need to have treated this more importantly in the public debate looms even larger because of the practical obligations it carries for American involvement in the reconstruction of Iraqi public order. The possibility of long-term American involvement should have been part of our general consideration of the argument for regime change, for political good typically does not come without some other political sacrifice. We should have—and always should—identified the goods and the sacrifices, then decided whether the sacrifices were worth making and, in practice, were likely to be made, given the other obligations our society has to its own people and to other nations. I think that these sacrifices have been worth making in the case of Iraq, and I would have had the Bush administration argue more forwardly for making this commitment in advance.

A related issue is the importance of involving other nations and international and nongovernmental organizations in securing the peace by rebuilding the society. This, more than their military contribution as such, is the most powerful argument for having a coalition of nations involved in actions to depose tyrannical regimes. After Bosnia, Kosovo, and Afghanistan, it was obvious that, in such cases, a relatively robust military presence is needed to maintain general order by deterring most outbreaks of force and punishing those which occur, coupled with a range of types of civilian activities aimed at reconstituting the society and establishing good government. These cases, especially the older ones from the former Yugoslavia, also show how difficult it is to carry this out and how much time and effort are required to succeed. Regime change is not accomplished merely by removing the evil regime; it also requires some such restorative process as this. The involvement of other states, of international and nongovernmental organizations, and of private voluntary organizations is, as the cases I have mentioned show, important for making this process work.

Another critical issue raised in the just war tradition and deserving of fuller reflection in the moral debate over using force against Saddam Hussein and his regime in Iraq is the requirement that a justified use of force ought to aim at establishing peace. Remarkably, all that this requirement might entail was utterly neglected in this moral debate. The aim of peace was certainly implicit in the administration's argument for the benefits—for Iraq, for the broader Middle East, and for the world—of establishing a free, democratic society in post–Saddam Hussein Iraq. But the subject of exactly how this would be accomplished within a society that had been systematically ravaged and demoralized for an entire generation did not enter into the debate. Arguments were put forward that looked back to Iraq's brief experience with democracy following the end of the British mandate, but they neglected to take into account the repression and systematic efforts at thought control characteristic of the intervening decades or the fact that many talented and independent-minded Iraqis had simply fled the country to escape this regime. Other arguments were put forward that emphasized the importance of personal liberty, as if freeing

Iraqis were all that would be needed, with a peaceful, democratic society directly following. Among the entries into the just war debate I have discussed in this chapter, only the Land letter actually touched on the importance of a peaceful Iraq, but it did so only indirectly, emphasizing the goal of establishing liberty:

> Liberty for the Iraqi people is a great moral cause, and a great strategic goal. The people of Iraq deserve it; the security of all nations requires it. Free societies do not intimidate through cruelty and conquest, and open societies do not threaten the world with mass murder.

Now, I certainly agree with this statement about the moral importance and the practical benefits of liberty. But liberty is not the only virtue of a good society. It must be exercised within a framework of order that disciplines individual liberty so that the strong do not once again prey on the weak, and it must be disciplined by a sense of justice in a way that makes personal liberty contribute to the common good of the society as a whole. The early modern political theorists spoke of the civic virtue needed for a free, democratic society to come into being and flourish. To speak of the importance of establishing liberty is an essential part of the moral whole, but there are other essential elements as well. Establishing liberty does not assure peace. Indeed, it may very well be the case, as I believe, that establishing at least a minimal peace is necessary for the exercise of genuine liberty.

Although speaking of establishing liberty was an essential part of the whole, the rest of what might be required for establishing a peaceful society in Iraq after the removal of Saddam Hussein and his regime simply was not addressed in the debate over whether to remove that regime by force. If we are to take seriously that a justified resort to force must intend the establishment of peace, then not addressing what this might mean in concrete terms is to miss an essential element in the just war idea. For the military and policy debates, to address this would have meant taking into account the reality that we confronted later: that U.S. military presence in Iraq would be required for an indefinite period after the actual defeat of Iraq's military forces and the overthrow of the Saddam Hussein regime; that perhaps more troops would be needed to establish and preserve order and the conditions for creating a free society than were required for the military defeat of the regime's forces in the first place; and that a significant presence of rebuilders of all sorts, as was the case in Bosnia and Kosovo, would be needed to help establish the conditions for a reconstituted, free, and democratic Iraqi society. The Bush administration, particularly the secretary of defense, has been repeatedly and energetically faulted for acting too unilaterally and for not having enough troops on the ground to establish and maintain order in post–Saddam Hussein Iraq. I share the concern about their not being enough troops to secure the peace, but as for the perceived unilateralism, this undertaking has never been so unilateral as its opponents have claimed, and even if it had, there are times when going it alone may be necessary if that is the only way to secure the right.

But why did the people I have discussed above not push for a discussion of the end of peace? That Bishop Gregory did not perhaps follows from his taking his cues from the conception of just war first laid out in *The Challenge of Peace*, which, with exquisite irony, did not include the end of peace in its listing of the requirements for a just war. Indeed, that document effectively defined peace as the absence of war, so there could be no place for the end of peace among the criteria for a just war—no matter what Augustine, Gratian, Thomas Aquinas, Francisco de Vitoria, and the just war tradition as a whole might have maintained. This is simply another example, and another very important one, of the lack of faithfulness to just war tradition embodied in the U.S. Catholic bishops' official position on the idea of just war. That the one hundred Christian ethicists did not discuss the end of peace but only stated their opposition to a preemptive war follows from the same assumption that peace means the absence of war, an assumption underscored by the presence of pacifists among the signatories. The position in the letter by Land and his associates, as I have already noted, addressed the goal of peace somewhat indirectly, as a product of liberty, but it focused on the establishment of liberty, not peace. As for the others that I have treated in this chapter, I offer no opinion as to why they did not urge the administration, in their moral reflection, to pay more attention to what would be necessary to secure the peace and to making this part of their own argument for justifying the use of force.

I must add myself to the list of those at fault for not trying to draw more attention to this aim of peace and the obligations that commitment to this entail. My position has been that the use of force to remove the Saddam Hussein regime was justified. I came to this position by a route that included the same two lines of reasoning that President Bush laid out in his second and third justifying arguments; indeed, I have thought the use of force to unseat Saddam Hussein and his regime justified since the aggression against Kuwait in 1990. The crimes of subsequent years only strengthened the case. But I have also, through this whole period, held to the position, in line with my understanding of the relationship between the classic deontological and contemporary prudential elements of the just war jus ad bellum, that even if the use of force is justified, it may not be wise, and it is far beyond my role as a moralist to make the call on the latter. As a private citizen, no matter how deeply I am engaged in the moral argument, I do not bear the responsibility of one in political authority, and only such a one, because of bearing that responsibility, has the right to make that decision. While I address the end of peace in a book I coauthored on the 1990–1991 Gulf War, I confess that I did not, during the 2002–2003 debate, see the importance of updating this earlier discussion and emphasizing the advance commitments implied by the requirement of aiming to establish peace. There is enough guilt here to go around. I believe we should have known better, that, if nothing else, the experiences of constructing peace in Bosnia and Kosovo should have led us to a more sophisticated and more demanding moral debate about aiming to create a peaceful society in Iraq. As I will argue further in the final chapter of this book, we need to learn from that and try to do better in the future.

A final note: like my teacher Paul Ramsey and the broad tradition of just war within which we both stand, I hold that there is a fundamental difference between the roles and competences of moralists and those in political responsibility. We moralists do not bear political responsibility, and in our reflection and in our advice, whether solicited or unsolicited, we need to take care that we do not act as if we do. The Land letter got this right, leaving the decision concerning resort to force with the political authority. But all citizens of a democratic society, including moralists, may rightly hold to account those who do bear the office of political responsibility to act according to that responsibility. The just war tradition of Western culture is about the achievement of peace—not just any peace but one characterized by a just political order, both within states and internationally, among states. It is a mistake to think of peace simply as the absence of war. Indeed, the use of armed force is properly a tool for good political leadership to use in the service of that fuller and more genuine peace. It is good or bad precisely as it intends to serve that goal or not. As the classic just war theorists well understood, the fundamental responsibility of those with sovereign authority is to serve a just and peaceful order. This is their particular burden. The justified use of force is one of the tools they must have available. To think otherwise is to forget the kind of world we live in.

**III**

# THE WAR TO OUST SADDAM HUSSEIN: DURING

# 4

# OPERATION IRAQI FREEDOM

## A Moralist's Notebook

It is one thing to reason abstractly about the moral justification and limitation of war; it is another to do so in the immediate context of a particular conflict. Operation Iraqi Freedom, with its unprecedented level of media coverage and the intimacy and immediacy provided by the reports of the journalists embedded in combat units, provided a unique opportunity to engage just war reasoning with day-by-day, case-by-case developments in the conduct of this extended battle. This chapter takes the form of a notebook or diary I began as Operation Iraqi Freedom was beginning. It focuses on particular incidents, identified by the press excerpts at the start of each section, as these incidents raise significant moral issues from the standpoint of the just war tradition. The chapter ends when the operation ended, with the taking of Baghdad.

### MARCH 19-21: DECAPITATION STRATEGY

*USA Today*, March 21–23, 2003, 1:
    U.S. military commanders in the Persian Gulf now may target Saddam Hussein without direct approval from the White House. . . .
    The shift of authority came a day after it took several hours for President Bush to approve a missile and bomb strike on a compound where the CIA believes Saddam was hiding in a concrete-enforced bunker.

71

During the night of Wednesday, March 19, before the formal start of the concerted air-ground assault called Operation Iraqi Freedom, an effort was made to kill Saddam Hussein and his two sons, Uday and Qusay, by a precision-guided missile and bomb strike at a bunker in Baghdad, where, according to intelligence received, the three were supposed to be spending the night. Such direct, intentional military targeting of the leadership of an enemy organization is called *decapitation*. The term may apply to the leadership of a terrorist or criminal organization or of military units or to critical officials at the top of a government against which military force is being used. The aim is to impair or destroy the ability of the organization in question to function.

Decapitation offers obvious benefits. In military terms, it holds out the possibility of achieving a desired end (lowering or wiping out the effectiveness of a military unit, for example) in a way that involves the limited use of resources, creates very limited collateral damage, is overall far less destructive than a broader use of military force would be, and may reduce the effort and cost of restoring the society in question after the conflict is over. In political terms, removing a despotic and tyrannical leader offers the opportunity both to punish that leader (by death) and to free the overall society to undertake political reform by means that involve limited risk and cost in resources and lives.

Decapitation also may be problematic both militarily and politically. In military terms, some kinds of fighting units may be prone to collapse if the top leadership is removed, but in other cases, decapitation may have adverse effects, like removing restraining discipline on the individual fighters or inspiring them to fight harder to avenge their dead leader. Also, a backup leader may immediately take over, stepping in for the leader who has been removed; provision for this is a standard element in military organization (the assistant squad leader, the platoon sergeant, the executive officer of a ship or a battalion). Political decapitation presents the same sorts of problems, in addition to some of its own. The secondary leadership may fragment, presenting the problem of a hydra-headed opposition in the place of one that appeared to have a single head. Settling the conflict may be difficult in such cases because if these rival power centers are not all dealt with individually, the result may be drawn-out fighting or even civil war. Another sort of problem arises from the degree to which political decapitation looks like assassination. For the United States, there is a particular problem: a long-standing series of presidential directives has forbidden assassination of foreign heads of state. So, the question of decapitation is not an easy one to answer, thinking in either military or political terms.

Similarly, in moral terms there are positive and negative aspects to decapitation. Within the frame of just war thought, one can argue that decapitation strategy is the best possible way of satisfying the ideal at which the principle of discrimination aims, targeting only those most responsible for carrying on the fighting, while in principle broadening the field of noncombatants to include all those who will not fight on after their leadership is removed. In terms of the principle of proportionality, too, decapitation seems to offer the prospect of less overall harm and destruction. A third consideration is that it may offer the most just response to injustice: in the case of a tyrannical leader guilty of horrible crimes, decapitation punishes that leader alone, without inflicting collateral harm on the innocent, including those who have already suffered much from the tyrant. And fourth, decapitation may be the most straightforward way to achieve a just, peaceful order. All of these lines of argument tend toward the conclusion that decapitation is a moral course of action, perhaps the most moral one among the options available.

But there are also negative considerations. The presidential directives forbidding the killing of foreign heads of state have an analog in the deep moral tradition against regicide, the killing of kings. Historically, this prohibition against regicide is linked to the idea that the sovereign ruler is chosen by God, so killing such a ruler violates the divine will. This is countered, though, by the similarly deep moral tradition that killing a tyrant (tyrannicide) is not the same as killing a king because the tyrant is not a legitimate ruler. So, in moral terms, the issue is not simply that of killing a head of state directly and intentionally; it is the legitimacy of a specific head of state in terms of whether he or she is carrying out, however well or badly, the responsibilities of sovereign authority or, to the contrary, is openly and egregiously violating those responsibilities, so that there is no doubt that he or she is in fact a tyrant, not a legitimate ruler. The bar needs to be high for making such a determination, for the decision as to whether decapitation is morally allowed is not one to make lightly. For this reason, it seems to me to be morally relevant that the initial decision to target Saddam Hussein and his sons required hours of deliberation; that the decision was not made quickly or lightly fits the deeply serious nature of the problem.

Another issue is that decapitation tends to make the use of force personal, whereas, in the just war tradition at least, the justified use of armed force aims at particular functions of the enemy, not the enemy's soldiers or their commanders, up to the level of the highest commander. This may be seen through the definition of noncombatant immunity, in which it is the function of involvement in the fighting that makes an individual a combatant and not being involved in fighting that makes one a noncombatant. For a significant period in the Middle Ages in western Europe, warriors after battle were required by church law to do penance before being readmitted to the sacraments—not because they might have killed other people or shed human blood, which was an assumed part of warfare, just or unjust, but because they might have done so out of wrong intention, including the desire to dominate others or a particular hatred toward another. That is, an important aim of the requirement of penance was to deal with the possibility that killing and maiming others in battle might have become personal. The ideal was to fight in a just cause impersonally, the way an executioner carries through what is required by public law without personal involvement. According to this model, decapitation is morally justified only if it aims at a particular function (as in the case of a strike against the leadership of a military unit) or if it aims to execute a particular punishment for crimes deserving such punishment (as in the case of a despotic ruler who has used state power to commit great crimes).

To carry this line of consideration further, whether decapitation raises moral problems may depend on the degree to which it looks like assassination. Decapitation accomplished as a result of a military action against a legitimate target may be justified as an act of war, while decapitation accomplished by stealth looks morally somewhat different; it looks like assassination, which in turn looks like murder, and to the degree that it looks like murder, it seems to have a different moral character from decapitation by military action. Murder is, of course, always wrong, by definition; yet not all killing, even when done by an individual and even when done by stealth, is murder. One can trace a long history of uneasiness over assassination in Western moral tradition, although the reasons are never fully clear. One problem is who engages in it: consider people like the Borgias, who carried out assassinations of their political enemies so as to gain and cement their own power. In just war terms, this is unjustified killing because they had no right to engage in it, both because they had no sovereign authority and because they did it for their private benefit. Another problem is the means: assassination is generally done by stealth and in private, while justified killing should be able to withstand the light of day. A third problem is that it may involve the use of criminals, people who regularly kill others for private gain. Viewed in terms of these problems, assassination looks like murder.

But the direct, intentional killing of an individual is not, by definition, murder. Killing in a just war is not murder, even when individuals are targeted, as by a sniper. Killing on public authority, as punishment for horrible crimes, is not murder. So, the issue of the morality of decapitation hinges on which of these two possible kinds of killing it is. And this, in turn, hinges on whether it satisfies the more general moral criteria for justified use of armed force defined in just war tradition: it must be undertaken on sovereign authority, for just cause, not out of wrong personal motivations but for the common good, including the aim of achieving peace, and its means must be discriminate and proportionate. As for the difference between overt military means and a covert operation, this difference in itself does not matter morally.

The switch to a policy allowing decapitation strikes against Saddam Hussein fits these criteria well. As commander in chief of the Iraqi armed forces, he is a legitimate combatant target. As perpetrator of well-attested atrocities against his own people and his neighbors, he has lost any protections due to sovereignty because these actions remove his legitimacy as ruler, and these atrocities open him up to punishment. Further, his is a special case: the decision to target him specifically (and to target others in leadership positions in his regime as well) does not negate the general principle that targeting heads of state is bad, for not all heads of state are like Saddam Hussein and not all are the objects of military action; in moral terms, this would be tyrannicide, not regicide.

## THE USE OF PRECISION-GUIDED MISSILES AND BOMBS

> *New York Times*, March 21, 2003, A1:
> A second wave of air attacks tonight against the strategic heart of the capital had all the eeriness and sudden, devastating power of modern high-technology warfare.
> The precision-guided bombs and missiles made at least two direct hits on a large, domed edifice beside the Tigris River. The building, possibly the planning ministry, exploded in a fireball and a series of secondary explosions.

During the public debate over the question of the use of armed force by the United States against Saddam Hussein's Iraq, I was invited to take part in a talk show based at the Chicago NPR station and syndicated on NPR. One of the questioners raised a question in the following terms: It is estimated that the U.S. will drop three thousand bombs and missiles on Iraq if it attacks. Assuming each one kills ten Iraqi people, then thirty thousand Iraqis will be the victims of the U.S. air assault. How could such losses from the Iraqi populace be justified?

This way of thinking about the use of military force I have found to be widespread among critics of its use. We saw it earlier in the case of President Carter's March op-ed article opposing the war. Carter wrote there, "The first stage of our widely publicized war plan is to launch 3,000 bombs and missiles on a relatively defenseless Iraqi population . . . with the purpose of so damaging and demoralizing the people that they will change their obnoxious leader."

Such an argument makes two assumptions: first, that bombing and missile strikes are by nature indiscriminate and, second, that the aim of such strikes is to kill members of the general populace of the nation under attack. Sometimes explicit and sometimes not is a third assumption: that the damage caused will be disproportionate to any reasonable calculation of the good achieved. There is a historical basis for such assumptions. First, they match the experience of strategic bombing as practiced in World War II and the so-called carpet bombing with "dumb" gravity bombs as late as the bombing campaign against Hanoi in the Vietnam War. (The use of such bombing by B-52s in the Gulf War of 1991 was directed at Iraqi armed forces, who by definition were combatants, and in this case discrimination was accomplished by the fact that the legitimate target was very large and deployed in an area where there were no noncombatants.) Second, the result, if not the theory, of strategic nuclear war would be large-scale loss of life and devastation of the societies targeted. If we think of the more general argument that modern warfare is inherently indiscriminate and disproportionate because of the nature of modern weapons, then this view of war actually goes back to the 1870s and the moral reaction against large-caliber rifled artillery capable of countercity bombardment from a distance. However we trace the roots of this understanding of warfare, though, it has become a staple of arguments against the use of military force. A version of it is to be found in the U.S. Catholic bishops' widely read pastoral letter of 1983, *The Challenge of Peace*, which argued that Catholic just war theory begins with a "presumption against war" that must be overturned if armed force is ever to be justified, and took the position, specifically with respect to nuclear weapons, that as a class, they can only be possessed as a deterrent but may never actually be used in a "war-fighting" way.

In the case of the moral opposition to the use of armed force against Saddam Hussein's Iraq, the argument focused specifically on the presumed effects of bombs and missiles armed with conventional warheads, but the lines of the argument were the same: these kill large numbers of the general populace and are intended to do so; thus, their use is immoral, and that makes the war itself immoral.

The assumption that the very nature of modern warfare is indiscriminate and disproportionate must be challenged. One problem is that it confuses the possession of great destructive power with how the available power is actually used. There are two things to say on this point. First, largeness is not in itself disproportionate. The just war criterion of proportionality requires a comparative measuring of the means to the end. The more important the end, the greater the destructive power that it is moral to use. Further, application of large amounts of force may in fact be the way to achieve the least amount of destruction. Such a tactic is common among police forces as a means of riot control: they blanket the riot-torn area with police to snuff out the rioting. In U.S. military usage, this tactic is known as the use of "overwhelming force." Critics do not acknowledge this, equating the application of large amounts of force to the intention of inflicting great and indiscriminate destruction. Their preference, assuming military force is used at all, would be to match force to force, offense to defense, as if combat were a more deadly form of a football game. Yet, fighting in such a way is more likely to create greater destruction and loss of life, for matchups of equal forces become extended firefights with high casualty rates. The moral criterion of proportionality, rightly used, does not require this but instead tends to support the overwhelming-force model of battle.

The second point to make about the confusion of the possession of destructive power with how that power is used is that the use of military force is not simply a function of the weapons available but always hinges on the choices made about how those weapons are used in particular circumstances. One should not, as the old saying goes, use a cannon to kill a mosquito. Yet, having a cannon in an area where there are mosquitoes does not mean that every time a mosquito is heard the cannon will be used. For every context in which military force is to be used, there are options. Humans must choose among the options, and here, in concrete instances, is where morality comes into play. The issue is how the available force is used, what choices are made among alternatives, and whether those choices use means that maximize discrimination and proportionality or not.

This assumes, of course, that the means available are not evil in themselves. Critics of modern warfare as inherently immoral seem to believe that all contemporary means of war are evil in themselves, when in fact there are serious differences. The idea of trying to limit the means of war by reference to the moral criterion of proportionality is comparatively recent, having come into the moral vocabulary on warfare only over the last forty years. Earlier just war thinking sought to limit the means of war by forbidding certain weapons as *mala in se*, or "evil in themselves." This is also the approach used in international law on war, the law of armed conflicts, which has accordingly sought to end the production, possession, and use of certain weapons, including weapons of mass destruction. From this perspective, there is a fundamental difference between using an outlawed means of war and one that is not. The former may never be used; use of the latter is subject to human choice and may not be indiscriminate and disproportionate.

Within the range of weapons not evil in themselves, there are always options, as argued above. But given the twin aims of avoiding harm to noncombatants and avoiding more destruction than necessary for a particular justified end, there is a moral obligation to develop weapons and tactics that better serve these ends and to incorporate these weapons and tactics into military training, operational plans, and combat decisions by commanders and individual soldiers. This, in moral terms, is the rationale for the development and adoption of precision-guided munitions (PGMs).

While estimates vary as to the number of noncombatant casualties caused by U.S. forces during Operation Iraqi Freedom, it is widely acknowledged that the use of PGMs enabled the destruction of the Iraqi regime's infrastructure and military capabilities with far lower levels of collateral harm than would have been the case with nonguided munitions and than was estimated by critics of the American use of force, including President Carter and the anonymous caller mentioned above. This had also been the case in Afghanistan, as well as in the strikes against Serbia over Kosovo—previous cases in which PGMs were used against targets in populated areas. The just war tradition stipulates that justified uses of force must proceed discriminately and proportionally but allows for collateral harm to noncombatants by the moral rule of double effect, which says that an action directly and intentionally aimed at a good may continue even though evil may result as an indirect, unintended effect of the action and provided that care is taken to try to minimize the bad effects. This allows in principle for a significant level of harm to noncombatant people and destruction of private and public property. The introduction and increasingly wide use of PGMs, part of what is called in military circles the "revolution in military affairs," changes all of the calculations.

First, such weapons are actually able to hit the legitimate targets at which they are aimed. In discussions of nuclear targeting, the circular error probable (CEP) became the standard measure of accuracy for a particular delivery system (missile or airplane-dropped bomb). This was the circle within which 50 percent of the weapons aimed at a particular target could be expected to fall. This meant in principle that for any given target, not one but two weapons would, at minimum, be needed. But there is more: the more hardened the target, the more destructive force needed to destroy it; at the same time, the larger the CEP of the weapon used, the more weapons needed to "fill" the circle and ensure the destruction of the intended target. The same term and the same reasoning, of course, could apply to nonnuclear armed missiles and bombs. This means that to destroy any given legitimate target, if the CEP is large, then many bombs or missiles will have to be used, and half of them may be expected to fall in the surrounding area, whether it is a legitimate (combatant) target or an illegitimate (noncombatant) object of collateral damage. To put this in plainer terms, the American bombers of World War II, using the Norden bombsight, which was the most accurate bombsight then available, might expect their bombs to fall within a box approximately one mile wide by five to seven miles long. (The size of the box would change given factors such as height, speed, visibility, and the bomber's need to take evasive actions, for even though the bombsight was intended to counteract such factors, in practice, greater height and speed increased the error on the ground, and evasive action, if fast, could not be compensated for accurately.) Although modern bombsights are more accurate, the nature of gravity bombs and their dependence on external conditions before and after their release means that they cannot hit a specific target within an area but must count on destroying the target while destroying the area. This is what leads critics of aerial warfare to regard it as being inherently about killing ordinary people (noncombatants) and destroying whole areas, such as cities. The development and use of precision-guided technology changes all of this radically. As in the newspaper report above, the aerial attack on the Ministry of Planning (a legitimate target) severely damaged the ministry while not damaging surrounding areas; the damage was held to the ministry building itself and the surrounding compound. The weapons fell where they were intended to fall.

Second, knowing that a weapon will hit the target aimed at means that less destructive power is needed to destroy a given target. If a given blast pressure is needed, a warhead that detonates immediately on target or even within a few yards of it may, in principle, be significantly less powerful than one that may fall fifty yards away. The diminution in destructive force needed is geometric, not linear, since blast pressure diminishes with the square of the distance. The result of increased accuracy in delivery systems is thus that significantly smaller warheads can be used to achieve the same desired effect, so that collateral effects outside the intended target are significantly decreased or eliminated.

Of course, weapons can still go off target. That is a different issue militarily, but it is the same morally: the result is unintended harm. There is a moral obligation to avoid using weapons with a high likelihood that they will go off target. Contemporary PGMs, though, have a very high success rate and correspondingly low failure rate.

Putting the matter simply, the development and deployment of precision-guided weaponry has radically changed the landscape of contemporary military operations and has also changed that of moral judgment about contemporary uses of armed force. This changed moral landscape means that moral judgments against contemporary warfare that assume its inherent indiscriminateness and disproportionality simply do not fit warfare carried on with PGMs, and it is time for critics of the use of military force to come to terms with this. It also means that in cases in which collateral damage can be avoided by use of PGMs, I believe any military that has them now has a moral obligation to use them. Occasions may still remain in which non-precision-guided weaponry may be used morally, for the old moral arguments relating to such weaponry still apply, but the moral preference for precision-guided weaponry is clear.

## AVOIDING HARM TO NONCOMBATANTS

> *New York Times*, March 22, 2003, D7:
> Civilian casualties are unavoidable in war, and this one is no exception. . . .
> But the U.S. military makes intense efforts to avoid civilian deaths. Washington trains its soldiers on the rules of war and has introduced procedures to try to minimize harm to noncombatants. The Defense Department's lawyers are constantly consulted about military strategy and targets when time permits; and the military has invested huge resources in developing precision-guided weapons to reduce the loss of innocent life. "It's an embedded and intrinsic part of American military culture post-Vietnam," said William Arkin, senior fellow at the Center for Strategic Education at Johns Hopkins University and senior military adviser to Human Rights Watch.

Avoiding harm to noncombatants is a fundamental element in using armed force morally. Moralists, increasingly over the last forty years, have referred to this as the principle of discrimination, but the older moral usage is to identify certain classes of people who are not to be the objects of direct, intentional harm in war because they do not normally, as a group, participate directly in military activities or engage in direct support of those activities. This is also the approach found in the law of armed conflicts, which has defined classes of "protected persons" (the language of the 1949 Geneva Conventions), including prisoners of war and military chaplains and medical personnel, as well as civilian noncombatants. In the 1977 Protocols to the Geneva Conventions, the term *civilians* was used to refer to noncombatants in general, and this usage is now widespread, although, technically, it is not accurate: civilians who take part in military activities, directly support them, or are involved in the chain of command for them are not noncombatants in fact, although in most conflicts, most civilians normally are.

Avoidance of harm to noncombatants is a matter of choosing among means, individual decisions by soldiers and commanders, tactics, strategy, and training. As noted above, respecting the moral requirements of seeking to avoid harm to noncombatants and seeking, more generally, to limit the destructiveness of war implies a moral obligation to develop means of high accuracy (so as to limit or eliminate collateral harm to noncombatants) and lowered destructive force (so as to limit overall destruction and, again, to limit or eliminate collateral harm to noncombatants). But these same two purposes also, and more immediately, call for education in the meaning of the restraints, formal programs of training, the effort to create what classically was called "virtue" (the habit of doing the right thing) in people involved in military service, and the development and use of tactics and strategies respecting these purposes. I suspect that comparatively few Americans among the general public, and even fewer non-Americans, have any idea of the truth of the statement by William Arkin above, or what this in fact means for how the American military is trained, organized, equipped, and led. The idea of just war, which in American civilian life is known and discussed only by a comparative few, is treated in the curriculum of all the service academies and the war colleges; lectures dealing with it and its application to contemporary military problems are frequent occurrences at such institutions, and presentations on it and its contemporary use have been a part of conferences organized by these institutions or their affiliated centers for military ethics. And beyond attention to the just war idea and its implications, all the services have programs of study and training oriented around the idea of ethics in military service. No other military in the world has a comparable level of institutionalized attention to ethics.

Yet, "civilian casualties are unavoidable in war, and this one is no exception." There is a vast moral difference, nonetheless, between a deeply rooted, conscious, and institutionalized effort to wage war so as to avoid or minimize such casualties and one that makes no such effort, recognizes no distinction between combatants and noncombatants, or, at the extreme, seeks intentionally to gain military advantage by putting noncombatants at risk or even directly, intentionally targets noncombatants. One example of the latter is treated in the next section; another sort of example is treated later. Where these divergent styles of warfare meet, there is pressure toward eroding the protection of noncombatants. In such a context, it is all the more important that this protection be maintained and that there be a deep institutional commitment to doing so.

## THE QUESTION OF JIHAD

*New York Times*, March 23, 2003, B13:
As Muslim preachers in the Gaza Strip inveighed today against war in Iraq as a war on Islam, leaders of the Palestinian group Hamas urged Iraqis to use suicide as a weapon against invading troops.
"As long as there is an American aggression against a Muslim country, Iraqis must defend themselves, using all means," Dr. Abdel Aziz Rantisi, a Hamas leader, said in a telephone interview from Gaza City.

The basis in Islamic law for such a position, as we saw in chapter 1, is a radical reading of an emergency provision allowed by the classical Muslim juristic authorities, who defined the idea of jihad—striving in the path of God—as including the use of armed force. These authorities, who lived during the early part of the Abbasid caliphate (the ninth and tenth centuries CE), understood the world in terms of two different and opposed realities, the House or Territory of Islam (*dar al-islam*), which consisted of that part of the world that submitted to God's law and was ruled by the caliph, the successor to the prophet Mohammad, and the House or Territory of War (*dar al-harb*), which consisted of the remainder of the world. This latter the Islamic jurists depicted as the source of all strife, due to its inhabitants' failure to accept God's law revealed through the Prophet. The House of War had no unity, they observed, and its various components were endemically at war with one another and with the House of Islam. Only in the latter was there true peace, which resulted from the organization of society according to the divine will and the submission of the members of that society to the divine law. On this basis, the jurists reasoned that opposing the House of War could be a religious duty, a form of jihad; yet, they set several stringent requirements for this.

First, they envisioned the normal form of such jihad as a community undertaking under the direction of the caliph, analogous to the early Muslim engagement in military activities under the leadership of the Prophet himself. Jihad understood this way was a "collective duty," a duty of the House of Islam as a whole. But a state of jihad against the House of War was not a continuous fact, according to the jurists' conception; rather, it was the caliph's place to declare jihad at a specific time of his choosing against a particular enemy from within the House of War; the caliph then raised and army and set up its command and supply structures. Within this conception, the jurists anticipated that there would be fighters and nonfighters, with the former drawn from among the able-bodied men of military age. While these would have the support of the community at large, the nonfighters in that community, even during jihad, would go about their normal lives. This conception was mirrored in what the jurists wrote about how Muslim fighters should conduct themselves when engaging in the jihad of collective duty: they should not target women, children, the aged, the infirm, or people engaged in religious calling (provided these belonged to the "people of the Book," that is, Christians and Jews). In short, the Islamic jurists conceived noncombatant immunity along lines similar to those of the just war tradition. They also set some limits on the means of warfare, although their major concern here was that Muslim armies should avoid the use of fire, understood to be the particular means God would use against the unrighteous in the last days. The conception of jihad thus defined was the normative conception.

However, the jurists also defined a second kind of jihad against the House of War, the jihad of individual duty. This was an emergency provision, a form of jihad that would be used as a kind of immediate, interim response to an invasion by an element of the House of War while the caliph mobilized the community response. If, for example, a family on the frontier of the House of Islam one day encountered an invading force from the House of War, its members' duty was not simply to report this to the caliph (although they should do that); it was also their duty as individuals to oppose the invading force to seek to slow it down or turn it back. This duty to oppose immediate aggression in the absence of a response under caliphal authority was the jihad of individual duty. It could not be the norm for the conduct of jihad because it suspended all the expectations and obligations of settled life in the House of Islam, including those established by divine law. In the jihad of individual duty, all have the obligation to fight, and they need permission from no one. Thus, not only the man of fighting age who heads the family and his sons of fighting age, but also the wife and daughters, the smaller children, and the aged and infirm, so far as they are able, have the same obligation and are not acting wrongly if they join in the fighting. The wife does not have to get her husband's permission; the son does not have to get his parents' permission; all may and must fight against the invaders. In fighting, moreover, no holds are barred: all of the invaders are, without exception, combatants, and they may be opposed by any means possible.

The exceptional character of this form of jihad, as conceived by the early Islamic jurists, must be stressed. The jurists, who after all began thinking about jihad in the sense of warfare by conceiving the House of Islam as the one place in the world in which social relationships and individual lives are rightly ordered, did not conceive of the jihad of individual duty as a normal, ongoing state of affairs. It was by definition a response to an emergency in the absence of a collective response undertaken by the leadership of the community, and as soon as that community response could be organized, the justification for jihad of individual duty disappeared.

Yet, contemporary radical Islam has remade the conception of the jihad of individual duty into a rationale for continuous warfare against America and the West, understood as the embodiment of the House of War. There are various pillars of this conception. Aggression against the House of Islam is defined as the presence not only of American or Western political or military power but also economic or cultural influence. Because any area that was at any time part of the House of Islam is properly still a part of it, American or Western presence in any such area is defined as aggression. As a corollary, any contemporary state in that area is properly "Muslim" and should be governed by a true Muslim and according to Muslim law. American or Western presence in any contemporary Muslim state is to be regarded as an aggression against all of the House of Islam to which all Muslims are obligated to respond, wherever they may be. Finally, this last proposition is usually transmuted into aggression against the religion of Islam, so that American or Western presence is represented as a religious assault. For all of these reasons, radical Islamists argue, in the current state of affairs, all true Muslims should regard themselves as in a condition of emergency, which obligates them to wage the jihad of individual duty against the aggressors. Such is the rationale Hamas has used for jihad against the state of Israel, which it has sought to demolish as a political entity and replace with an Islamic government, and such is the rationale al Qaeda has used to justify its attacks against the United States. This is also the rationale that leads to the specific call for jihad against the United States for its military presence in Saudi Arabia and now for its use of military force in Iraq. Suicide bombing, the tactic used by al Qaeda and by Hamas against Israel, is redescribed as a "martyrdom operation" in this present-day jihad of individual duty.

This radical Islamist doctrine differs importantly from the classical Islamic juristic conception of the emergency jihad of individual duty and, in important ways, conflicts with it. The jurists conceived of a particular military intrusion in a remote place that created a specific, limited, temporary justification for abrogating the usual rules of social life and for using armed force. All of the intruders were by definition combatants and could be treated as such. Although one might fight heroically at the risk of death, actions aimed specifically at martyrdom were forbidden, as the jurists understood martyrdom to be forbidden in Muslim law. The jurists' House of Islam was also a specific place, with territorial boundaries and a common political community inside those borders. The radical conception differs on all these points. Its conception of the Muslim world takes no account of the reality that the House of Islam, in its legal sense, does not exist and has not existed for a long time. Its conception of the "aggression" offered by non-Muslim societies and cultures is not particular but general; it is more like the juristic assumption of the difference between the House of Islam and the House of War than the particular aggression the jurists had in mind to create a situation of emergency. The radical conception is of a long-term, perhaps even perpetual, state of the jihad of individual duty, not one limited in duration and space. And because of their fuzzy, but global, idea of what constitutes aggression and who the aggressors are, the radicals treat all of the enemy as combatants, as both al Qaeda and Hamas practice demonstrate.

Although the use of suicide bombing against the American armed forces in Iraq began shortly after this call to jihad and suicide missions, it has grown in the aftermath of the conflict itself and the fall of the Saddam Hussein regime. The suicide bombing of the U.N. headquarters in Baghdad on August 19, 2003, was, from the radical perspective, only a tactical, not a fundamental, shift in doctrine: the United Nations is itself part of the culture arrayed aggressively against the House of Islam; its workers in Baghdad, although unarmed civilians in noncombatant relief roles, were thus, by definition, combatants and deserved to die. The radicals' view of the world is of an ongoing, fight-to-the-death clash of civilizations, which justifies extreme measures and ultimately knows no limits as to means or targets. No compromise is possible. Theirs is a view deeply at odds with that of Islamic tradition, but by co-opting and redefining the concept of strife between the House of Islam and the rest of the world and that of the emergency jihad of individual duty, the radicals have cloaked their cause and the methods they use in an appeal to ultimate religious truth. Defeating them is thus as much a matter of removing that cloak as it is of containing and suppressing them by police and military efforts.

## ERODING NONCOMBATANT PROTECTION AS A WAR-FIGHTING POLICY

> *The Star-Ledger* (Newark, New Jersey), March 24, 2003, 1:
> Headline: "Iraqis Fake Surrender and Put Prisoners on TV"
> By ambush and faked surrender, Iraqi forces killed, wounded, and captured Americans—and some of them, alive and dead, were exhibited on Iraqi television.
> Marines encountered Iraqi troops who appeared to be surrendering. Instead, the Iraqis attacked.

> *New York Times*, March 24, 2003, B6:
> Reports of Iraq's tactics on the battlefield and its treatment of captured Americans were seen by U.S. officials as evidence of serious violations of international conventions on the conduct of war. . . .
> Coalition officials . . . reported that Iraqi forces had fought out of uniform, had flown false flags of surrender and then attacked, and had massed civilians to shield themselves from attack, all considered violations of the codes of war.

Maintaining the protection of noncombatants is one of the critical moral goals in the use of military force. When only one side seeks to do this, or when one side uses the other's commitment to maintain this protection as a way to gain military advantage, then the protection itself is made more difficult and may be eroded in practice, even when there is a continuing commitment to it.

The above headline and excerpts from newspaper stories reflect the first instances in what turned out to be a continuing practice by members of the Fedayeen Saddam and other paramilitary groups to gain military advantage over the American and British troops by various means involving the commitment of those troops to maintaining the protection of noncombatants. In one instance, reported in a story cited above, Iraqi combatants feigned surrender, then took up hidden weapons and fired on the approaching Americans. In other instances, Iraqi combatants disguised themselves as civilians, then, when close to American soldiers, took out weapons and fired on them. In Basra, defending Iraqi fedayeen drove civilians out before them as human shields so as to attack the British soldiers seeking to take that city, and on another occasion, the fedayeen fired on a large group of civilians, including women and children, who were crossing a bridge to take refuge with the British soldiers. Of a different, but related, character was the other incident related in the above headline and stories, the Iraqi effort to gain advantage by exhibiting on television captured and dead American soldiers.

It is important to understand first that all of these are related in moral terms. A noncombatant is anyone who does not take a direct part in military activities or give direct support to such activities. Standard lists of noncombatants in the moral tradition include women, children, the aged, the infirm, and people whose social role or occupation does not include such involvement (like farmers on the land, merchants, teachers, and clergy). Beginning with the first Geneva Convention of 1864, international law on armed conflicts has also extended noncombatant protection to military personnel rendered *hors de combat* by reason of being wounded or taken prisoner, and it has made explicit that military chaplains and medical personnel, although in uniform, are noncombatants also. So, in practice, all of these groups are to be extended protection as noncombatants (although the specific rules for treatment of civilians and military personnel in the named categories differ). Degrading treatment of enemy prisoners of war and enemy dead is forbidden; this is interpreted in the law as meaning not only physical abuse but also psychological stress, including exhibiting them for propaganda purposes. The underlying theme is that the forbidden treatment is such that it undermines the protection due the affected people as noncombatants.

While the other sorts of actions I have mentioned are each different in their particulars, they all share this characteristic. When combatants pretend to surrender in order to gain military advantage, the effect is to undermine the protection due to combatants who are genuinely surrendering; as a result, they may be fired upon or treated more harshly on capture. When combatants pretend to be civilians to gain military advantage, it undermines the effort to maintain noncombatant protection for civilians, for civilians, as a category, may become suspect. Although the commitment to keep from harming such people may remain, carrying this through in practice inevitably becomes more difficult, and mistakes may be made that were less likely before. An example is the case of the first car bomber who attacked American forces south of Baghdad;

later, cars containing civilians who were really noncombatants were fired on because they did not understand the orders to stop, thus were mistaken as involved in another car-bombing attempt.

The incidents at Basra are of still another sort, although, again, they share a common theme with the others I have been discussing. Intentionally using civilians as shields turns them into people operating in direct support of the military effort of those who are using them in this way. Since the traditional moral and legal understanding of combatancy and noncombatancy hinges on whether the people in question function as combatants or in direct support of the combat operation, not on whether they do so voluntarily, people being used involuntarily as human shields are, formally speaking, not noncombatants any more, and they may be fired upon. At the same time, if the opposing force is committed to avoiding direct, intended harm to particular classes of people who are normally noncombatants, they cannot help observing that the human shields are not there of their own volition, and this creates a motivation to try to fire around them at the combatants who are using them. The problem is that, in this kind of situation, it may be hard not to harm the human shields. Those who are driving the human shields before them are seeking an immediate military advantage, but they are also seeking a propaganda victory, for if the enemy troops kill or wound any of the human shields, this can be presented as evidence that the enemy does not respect noncombatant life. For the Iraqi forces themselves to fire directly on civilians attempting to escape and take refuge obviously makes those forces themselves guilty of any harm that comes to the noncombatants, but those forces are also properly guilty if any harm comes to noncombatants they are using as human shields. This is often hard for people who oppose any killing in war to grasp, but these two types of cases are fundamentally the same morally. Respect for noncombatant protection means that it is wrong to directly, intentionally endanger noncombatants in a combat situation. At the same time, even in the face of actions that undermine or flout such protection, there remains an obligation to seek to honor it; thus, the importance of efforts to inculcate a deep respect for such protection.

On the day of the events reported above, I was watching a CNN report in which the reporter sought a reaction from an American soldier: "We have learned that the Iraqis have been mistreating captured Americans. Does that mean that the Americans are now going to start mistreating captured Iraqis as well?" The American soldier looked at the reporter somewhat incredulously for a finite moment, then replied, "Of course we won't. That's not who we are." This is an example of what I referred to earlier as virtue, the habit of doing the right thing. More specifically, this incident reveals the classic virtue of fortitude, doing the right thing in the face of adversity. Ethical conduct in war requires such virtue.

## THE PROBLEM OF IRREGULAR WARFARE

> *New York Times*, March 26, 2003, B5:
> Headline: "Army Failed to Anticipate the Attacks by Irregulars"

The Iraqi regular military forces arrayed against the American and British were part of the Iraqi Army, which was large and, especially in the case of the Republican Guards units, well equipped with tanks and other weapons, well trained, and highly motivated. The Saddam Hussein government, however, made a policy decision to employ irregular forces against the coalition troops, while the regular forces largely melted away as their fighting power was systematically destroyed by superior American power and tactics, including precision targeting of Iraqi armor from the air. The Iraqi irregulars were various paramilitary or militia bodies that had originally been created and used to underpin the regime by serving as spies and enforcers against the population, especially the Shia in the south. They were well armed with hand weapons, rocket-propelled grenades, and, in some cases, tanks. They were also highly motivated and disciplined, but their discipline was not in following the laws of armed conflict or respect for internationally recognized human rights; rather, corresponding to their original function as enforcers for the regime, their discipline was oriented in just the opposite direction.

Irregular forces are not a new phenomenon. One term for irregulars, *guerrillas*, comes from the Napoleonic campaign in Spain early in the nineteenth century, when members of the Spanish population staged hit-and-run attacks against the French supply route and against small units of French army regulars. This irregular warfare was called *guerrilla*, literally "little war" (from the Spanish *guerra* for "war"), and the irregular forces who waged it were called *guerrilleros*. Later the term *guerrilla* was applied to the fighters themselves, and their style of war was called "guerrilla warfare." By the time of the American Civil War, another term, *partisan*, was in general use in legal and military circles. This was the term employed (with a nod to "guerrilla warfare" as carrying the same meaning) by Francis Lieber, the international lawyer commissioned by the U.S. Army to write a study on partisan warfare in 1862 and, the next year, to serve as the principal drafter of what became *General Orders No.*

*100 (1863): Instructions for the Conduct of Armies of the United States in the Field*, the forerunner both of modern military manuals on the laws of war and of modern rules of engagement. The term *partisan* has given way in recent usage to the term *irregular*, and I will use these terms interchangeably below.

In the Civil War, there were many self-constituted partisan groups on both sides of the conflict, and while some of them behaved responsibly, others behaved essentially as bandit gangs. Lieber laid down a series of tests to determine whether a partisan band should be treated as legitimately engaged in military activities, thus whether its members were to be treated as soldiers in combat if captured or as spies or criminals. The members of a partisan group, according to these standards, should carry out their operations subject to higher military discipline and behave in a manner showing respect for such discipline, and while not required to wear military uniforms, they should wear some distinguishing mark or sign (e.g., a particular type of hat, a specific color of shirt or coat, or a colored armband), carry their arms openly, and fight according to the "laws and customs of war," which at that time did not yet refer to positive law, which had not yet been codified, but to the consensus on these laws and customs to be found in the work of theorists of international law, including Lieber himself. (In the 1863 *Instructions*, these laws and customs were laid down as legal requirements for the conduct of the U.S. Army.) Lieber's standards for partisan warfare almost immediately began to have a wide influence, and in the Annex to 1907 Hague Convention IV, they were internationally adopted as part of the regulations to be observed in land warfare. Later, these four criteria became part of the 1949 Geneva Conventions and, with two important changes, were reiterated in the 1977 Geneva Protocols. Those changes were to weaken the requirements that legitimate partisans wear a distinctive sign to distinguish themselves from the general population and carry their arms openly. The conditions set by the 1949 Geneva Conventions included "that of having a fixed distinctive sign recognizable at a distance" and "that of carrying arms openly"—both restatements of the criteria laid down by Lieber and used in the Hague Convention. The language of the 1977 Protocols, though, was significantly vaguer and less restrictive:

> Recognizing . . . that there are situations in armed conflicts where, owing to the nature of the hostilities an armed combatant cannot so distinguish himself, he shall retain his status as a combatant, provided that, in such situations, he carries his arms openly (a) during each military engagement, and (b) during such time as he is visible to the adversary while he is engaged in a military deployment preceding the launching of an attack in which he is to participate. (1977 Protocol

1, Article 43. Protocol 1 deals with international armed conflicts. Protocol 2, which deals with noninternational armed conflicts, does not treat this subject.)

The upshot of this language is to weaken the criteria severely. By it, combatants do not have to wear uniforms or any other distinguishing sign when "the nature of the conflict" prevents it, and they do not have to carry their arms openly until they are actually "engaged in a military deployment preceding the launching of the attack." This language opens the door to two unfortunate results: that irregular forces may push the limits of what is allowed by the Protocols to gain military advantage, and that by doing so, they may undermine the protection of noncombatants, as already discussed. The United States has signed but not ratified the Protocols. Official U.S. policy is to observe those elements of the Protocols that are part of customary international law. Arguably, this means the state of the law at the time of the 1949 Conventions, which employ the original language of the conditions for legitimate partisan warfare. Iraq has neither signed nor ratified the Protocols; however, it ratified the 1949 Conventions, signaling its intention to be bound by them.

The effort to define what constitutes legitimate participation in warfare by partisan or irregular forces has two opposite aims: assimilating the treatment of legitimate irregulars—those who fight in accord with the standards laid down—to that of regular forces, both in combat and in situations when they are taken prisoner, and clarifying the illegitimacy of those irregulars who do not fight according to these standards. The former are legitimate combatants, to be treated the same as uniformed members of regular forces, while the latter are illegitimate or illegal combatants, who are not entitled to such treatment and are, in effect, criminals. This is why the behavior of irregulars in combat is critical. How they behave in combat determines how they should be viewed, morally as well and legally, and how they should be treated in combat and if captured. That the Iraqi irregulars violated these conditions was their crime, not that they were irregulars per se.

While the idea of rules for war may seem counterintuitive to many people, in fact all major cultures have moral traditions (such as the just war tradition of the West) that seek to define such rules, and since the 1860s, a significant body of positive international law—originally called the law of war, now called the law of armed conflicts—has come into existence with the purpose of seeking to regulate and limit the conduct of armed conflicts. This body of law, as already indicated in discussions in other contexts above, contains protections for noncombatants and sets limits on the means of war, doing so through a variety of international conventions, declarations, and protocols. But unlike domestic laws, international law has no supreme governing body to enforce it; rather, its binding power depends on the degree to which the governments and armed forces of the world are committed to observing it in practice when in situations of armed conflict. Having signed the international agreements in question is not enough; more important is what is done in practice. What nations do in practice is termed *customary law*, and so, the ideal is to have the positive law and the customary law coincide. Enforcement of the positive law is then possible through the weight of the consensus among those governments and armed forces committed to observing it as their customary practice. Such enforcement may take the form of diplomatic suasion, threats, or the imposition of various sanctions or may entail more extreme measures, such as use of military force or war crimes trials for the offenders. Nonetheless, such enforcement is not always effective, especially when many sympathize with the offenders. Enforcement is also difficult to achieve when one or both parties to an armed conflict are irregular forces, as is normally the case in civil wars; it is essentially impossible to achieve when one or both parties to the conflict define their aims in terms of some transcendent ideal or irreconcilable hatred for the enemy, so that the conflict is understood as all-or-nothing. Recent armed conflicts provide numerous examples of armed forces that have fought without regard for the legal restraints or the underlying base of moral restraints.

The problem in such warfare is thus twofold: first, how does one restore respect for the limits laid down in the law of armed conflicts and in the deeper moral tradition among those who violate them; second, what should the opposing force do when the enemy flouts the rules to gain military advantage?

Asymmetrical warfare, that between opposing forces of significantly different sizes or capabilities, often provides a further rationale for fighting without regard to legal or moral restraints. The less militarily powerful side puts forward the argument that the playing field is not level and that if they fight according to the rules, they have no chance of defending themselves against their opponents or prevailing over them. At the same time, they do not accept that their better armed and trained or more numerous opponents have the right to use similar methods against them: in short, the argument is that the less powerful side has the right to fight without regard for restraints, while the more powerful side must observe all the restraints. The legal and moral answer is that the restraints must be observed, but by both sides. Failure to do so, in the case of irregular forces, opens them up to being treated not as legitimate combatants but as criminals guilty of many violent crimes; failure to do so on the part of regular forces makes them, in principle, subject to war-crimes investigations, trials, and punishments. Asymmetry is no excuse for violating the accepted rules, which give soldiers going into combat an understanding of what to expect of their adversaries.

## COLLATERAL DAMAGE, ACCIDENTS OF WAR, AND INTENTIONAL ACTIONS: NOT ALL HARM TO NONCOMBATANTS IS MORALLY THE SAME

> *New York Times*, March 27, 2003, A1:
> Two large explosions detonated simultaneously in a working-class district of Baghdad this morning, killing 17 civilians and wounding 45 others, hospital officials said.

In response to the incident reported above, Iraqi officials immediately blamed American bombs or missiles. American officials, while saying that they did not really know the cause, said that there were no planned strikes in the area and that no planes had been there. They added that Iraqi agents wearing American uniforms and strapped with explosives had been working in the area, so the blasts might have been an intentional effort to direct popular blame toward the American forces. Journalists reporting from the blast site observed that the craters were only a fraction of the size of those made by American bombs. Later, there was speculation that the blasts were caused by errant Iraqi antiaircraft missiles falling back to earth.

The term *fog of war* covers many things about which not enough is known with certainty. To my knowledge, the exact cause of these blasts was never determined. It is clear, though, that the various possible explanations are of different moral character. All harm to noncombatants, regrettable though it is, is not morally the same. I will distinguish three kinds of possible explanations and how they look morally.

- *Explanation 1:* The blasts were caused by direct American bomb or missile strikes aimed at the sites in question, which were market areas in built-up civilian neighborhoods. Such strikes would violate the moral and legal prohibition against direct, intentional harm to noncombatants. Given the overall American policy of attempting to avoid such harm, together with ample evidence of the U.S. ability to do so, this is an unlikely cause of the blasts.
- *Explanation 2:* The blasts were caused by American bombs or missiles

that had gone astray or by Iraqi antiaircraft missiles falling back to earth. If something of this sort caused the blasts, then the cause would be an accident of war, an unintended accidental effect of an acceptable military action. Such accidental damage is often linked in the public mind with collateral damage (the lists of civilian casualties do not normally sort out their cause), but they are different. Collateral damage is harm caused by the effects of a strike on a legitimate military target on noncombatants who happen to be in the area of the target. It can (and should) be minimized, as noted above, by using weapons of high accuracy and warheads of limited destructive power ("low yield"). Accidental damage is harm caused by a weapon that goes astray: it may have been fired unintentionally; it may have been aimed at a legitimate target, but for some reason (including enemy defensive fire), its guidance mechanism went awry; it may have failed to explode in the area of the intended target but detonated when it fell back to earth, as in the case of antiaircraft missiles; finally, the weapon may have been wrongly aimed because of the fog of war. While there is arguably a moral obligation to seek to minimize such accidents (doing so also follows from military efficiency), accidents are by definition events that happen because of a loss of control. If the blasts in question were accidental, whatever the immediate cause, that would be very different, morally, from blasts that were intended.

- *Explanation 3:* The blasts were caused by Iraqi agents working covertly. Like the first possible explanation considered above, this means that the blasts were direct, intended attacks on noncombatants. Doing such harm to noncombatants is equally wrong, whoever does it. But if in this case the blasts were the work of Iraqi covert agents, then there is a further moral fault: a government has an obligation to serve its people's good; instead to attack them directly and intentionally flouts that obligation.

Noncombatants, as well as combatants, get injured and killed in armed conflicts. But there is a real moral difference between harm done directly and intentionally to noncombatants and harm that is collateral to a legitimate military action or harm that is accidental. In both of these latter cases, there is an obligation to take steps to avoid such harm; yet, in some cases, it is unavoidable. The mere fact that such harm happens does not entail moral guilt for it.

## CRIMINAL WAYS OF FIGHTING

*New York Times*, March 27, 2003, A1, B4:
Headline: "Iraqi Soldiers Say It Was Fight or Die"

"The officers threatened to shoot us unless we fought," said a wounded Iraqi from his bed in the American field hospital here [Diwaniya]. . . .

"I have four children at home, and they threatened to hurt them if I did not fight," another one of the wounded Iraqis said. "I had no choice."

*New York Times*, March 27, 2003, B4:
Headline: "Trying to Sort Out the Enemy from the Innocent Passer-by"

The fighters have dressed as civilians, pretended to be civilians trying to surrender and have used schools and hospitals as headquarters during the battle. . . . They have hidden weapons all over town, so that in case they are stopped, they are unarmed. . . .

As a result, all civilians around Nasiriya are suspect.

*New York Times*, March 27, 2003, B12:
Headline: "Urban Warfare: Long a Key Part of an Underdog's Down-to Earth Arsenal"

"[Urban warfare] tends to become a low-tech, house-to-house situation, and that kind of combat can become very costly for combatants and others." A war depending on low technology and high numbers of . . . casualties is the opposite of what most of the modern American Army is trained to do.

*New York Times*, March 27, 2003, B7:
Who is a fedayeen fighter and who is a civilian? Marines tell stories of Iraqis changing in and out of uniform. A civilian bus turns out to be a troop transport. Guerrillas cluster near schools and hospitals. In several cases, troops carrying white flags have opened fire. Iraqis do not play by the rules of West Point and Sandhurst.

In Frederick the Great's armies, the noncommissioned officers went into battle behind the main line of battle (the officers were out front, as visible signs of their leadership). Their job was to spur the troops on when they encountered difficulty, and to kill any who tried to run. Paul Fussell, in *The Great War and*

*Modern Memory*, tells a story of a British officer near the front who encountered several British soldiers deserting the trenches. The officer later reported that he shot and killed all of the men except one, with the result that the desertion was ended. Such actions rightly make one's blood run cold, and they should do so whether the force in question is a major power, as were both Frederick's Prussia and World War I–era England, or a lesser, but still militarily potent, power like Saddam Hussein's Iraq.

The Saddam Hussein regime (or more properly, Saddam Hussein himself, since his word was law) apparently had decided before the beginning of the coalition assault that it would use means that are outlawed in the law of armed conflicts and deeply immoral by the standards of Islamic tradition as well as just war. The aim was to gain military advantage, both tactically—that is, in terms of the immediate firefight—and strategically—that is, by seeking to draw the coalition forces into the same kind of fighting in order that this could be used against them for propaganda purposes. To force soldiers into fighting on threat of immediate death short-circuits legitimate means of military discipline and amounts to unlawful coercion and murder. To do so by threatening the children of soldiers is heinous in its own right, for the same reason that murdering noncombatant hostages is legally and morally wrong. For combatants to pretend to be civilians or to use legally protected places as bases not only confers unfair advantage, but it directly contravenes and tends to erode noncombatant protection. Finally, doing so in the context of urban warfare, which vastly increases the opportunity for using noncombatants as human shields, pretending to be noncombatants for military advantage, and using civilian houses as well as protected places like hospitals and schools, raises all this to a higher power. These are criminal means of waging war, forbidden both in international law and in moral tradition.

The obligation to seek to avoid noncombatant casualties remains. The problem is how to fight according to this obligation when the opponent is intentionally fighting either without regard to high noncombatant casualties or, as in the case of the Iraqi irregulars, is apparently seeking either to increase them to a level that coalition troops will find intolerable or to add to the strength of the opposition to the coalition's use of force and stop it in this way. Soldiers have an obligation to seek to minimize noncombatant casualties and ought never to attack noncombatants directly and intentionally. But this does not mean that they have no obligation to protect themselves or their fellows or to seek to fight the enemy effectively. The answer to the question of how to fight against an enemy who uses unlawful and immoral means has two dimensions. The first dimension is advance preparation of the soldiers. Their training should be aimed at instilling a sense of self based on moral strength (virtue), which leads them, from deep inside, to seek to protect noncombatants and to be revolted by tactics that intentionally endanger them or sacrifice their lives for military advantage. At the same time, this advance training should also include specific preparation for situations in which the enemy uses noncombatants in the ways described above, so that those who use these tactics can be countered and overcome without resorting to the same means they use. The second dimension is the use of overwhelming power against those who fight criminally, thus changing the context so that they cannot use these methods or benefit from them. It is not necessary to use immoral means to respond to the use of immoral means; here, as in other kinds of situations, the best defense is a good offense.

"Iraqis do not play by the rules of West Point and Sandhurst." One may go in a number of different directions from a statement like this. One way would be to argue that the rules of West Point and Sandhurst (actually, the law of armed conflict and of moral tradition) should be forgotten in the face of the Iraqis' use of illegal and immoral methods. But to do this in pursuit of tactical victory is in fact to give strategic victory to the policy of using such methods, for breaking down coalition discipline in that way is one of the aims of this means of fighting. And, as I have already argued, to do so would be to betray the coalition soldiers' sense of self and purpose, as well as the aims for which they are fighting. Another direction one could go in from the above quotation is to argue that all war is necessarily all-out. This is a frequent theme found among both pacifists and advocates of total war as policy; both believe that rules and restraints have no place in armed conflict—pacifists because they want to argue that war is inherently so horrible that the only possible restraint is simply not to engage in it; total-war advocates because they believe that the aim of victory creates its own morality and that fighting according to legal or moral restraints interferes with the achievement of victory. These attitudes are equally far from the insistence on restraints found in the law of armed conflicts and in the just war tradition. The study of this law and this moral tradition and their incorporation into the kinds of training described above makes possible a kind of fighting that proves both the pacifists and the advocates of total war wrong. Finally, one may read the above quotation simply as a statement of fact, which it is. It implies nothing about the need for coalition forces to disregard the rules. At the same time, it serves as a pithy reminder that under the stress of combat in which the enemy uses criminal means, it is necessary to have well-trained troops with a deep sense of self, operating in numbers and with tactics that allow them to counter the advantages gained by the enemy through their illegal and immoral means.

## THE EFFECTS OF BOMBING: THREE KINDS OF CASES

*New York Times*, March 29, 2003, A 1:
Iraqi officials said tonight that at least 35 people, possibly as many as 55, many of them women and children, were killed when a missile or bomb struck a crowded marketplace in an impoverished district of Shiite Muslims in the northwest suburbs of Baghdad. Dozens of others were wounded, many of them critically. . . .
But as with another similar incident on Wednesday, when two explosions in another working-class district of Baghdad killed at least 17 people and wounded 45, it was impossible to determine the cause.

*New York Times*, March 29, 2003, B3:
Tonight, a huge bomb struck in the area beside the Tigris River where the Information Ministry is situated, and initial reports indicated that the ministry had been substantially damaged, or even destroyed. The Pentagon had warned for weeks that Western reporters should stay away from the ministry, since it was a potential target as a telecommunications and propaganda center.

*New York Times*, March 29, 2003, B5:
Nearly 40 Apache helicopters from the Army's 101st Airborne Division attacked part of the Iraqi Republican Guard's Medina Division today. . . . The helicopters in tonight's attack often worked as a lure, drawing fire from the ground and establishing targets that were then struck by American and British air forces and by rocket-propelled artillery.

The above reports illustrate three different kinds of effects from bombing. The first, as discussed in connection with the earlier case from March 27, would violate noncombatant immunity if it were intentional. This would be the case whether it was the result of an intentional air strike or an intentional act by Iraqi irregulars to seek to blame the American bombing campaign for propaganda purposes. As in the earlier case, though, the prima facie evidence suggests that it was accidental, either an American missile gone astray or an Iraqi antiaircraft missile that fell back to earth and then exploded. Accidents of war, while regrettable and to be avoided so far as possible, are not at all the same, morally or legally, as intentional attacks.

The second and third reports above describe the use of aerial bombing against two morally and legally different kinds of targets. That described in the last report is an unambiguous use of aerial bombing (and other forms of force) against a military target engaged in battle. Such targeting, in terms of both just war reasoning and the law of armed conflicts, is entirely allowed. The only restraints have to do with means: they must be proportionate (that is, not cause more harm than necessary to achieve the justified result, which in this case would be to degrade or destroy the Medina Division's combat effectiveness) and not use prohibited weapons, weapons deemed to be *mala in se*.

Under certain circumstances, these last two approaches to limiting means are in conflict. During the Vietnam War, moralist Paul Ramsey published an article arguing for the moral preferability, in terms of the criterion of proportionality, of incapacitating gases over the alternatives, which included high volumes of bullets, high-yield explosives, and napalm (*The Just War*, 465–78). Ramsey was speaking specifically of the question of how to deal with Vietcong forces in tunnel complexes; he suggested that in such a situation, the use of an incapacitating gas would not raise the problem of indiscriminateness normally characteristic of gas warfare and that the proper kind of incapacitant could allow the combatants in the tunnels to be taken prisoner without being killed. The problem, of course, is that the international legal ban on gas warfare arguably includes incapacitants, so even if an incapacitant could be devised that did in fact produce the desired end—flushing the combatants from the tunnels or incapacitating them harmlessly within the tunnels so that they can be taken prisoner—it would be illegal. This example shows clearly that the two approaches found in moral discourse and the law—argument from the principle of proportionality and argument from restraints or prohibitions directed at specific means—do not necessarily lead to the same conclusion.

Another example illustrating the same tension comes from Lieber's notes during the American Civil War. Lieber, remembered as an apostle of restraint in war, kept notes showing a fascination with new or unusual weapons, particularly the exploding bullet, and with the effort by Confederates to start a cholera epidemic in New York by means of a clandestine shipment of infected blankets. His notes show that he was attracted to such means as ways that might shorten the war, thus reduce the overall cost in human lives. Exploding and expanding bullets were later explicitly forbidden by 1899 Hague Declaration 3 and are currently banned by the 1980 U.N. Protocol on Non-Detectable Fragments. Making war by attempting to spread disease is the general topic addressed legally first by the 1925 Geneva Protocol that prohibited bacteriological warfare (the same protocol that originally prohibited gas warfare) and currently disallowed by the 1972 Biological Weapons Convention.

To put the matter of this disagreement more generally, the U.S. military makes its decisions regarding means first of all in terms of whether the means in question are legally allowed; it only brings considerations of proportionality into the decision later on, and then only in hard cases in which there are clear choices of alternatives. Proportionality used in this way becomes a kind of calculation of relative military effectiveness—what will be the cost on both sides of a particular choice of means versus an alternative choice. For moralists who rely entirely on the principle of proportionality, the aim is generally to use the least destructive means. Ramsey's argument shows how this can lead to a preference for incapacitating weapons, even if they are of a sort that would violate international law. But this sort of case would be unusual. More generally, the moralists who use the principle of proportionality alone tend to be uneasy about significant destructiveness in itself. Their approach thus pushes, in principle, toward the development and use of ever smaller and more closely targeted means, whereas approaching the question of means through the question of what is prohibited and what is licit carries no such implications. In practice, what is allowed in the latter terms may be criticized as disproportionate in the former terms.

In my judgment, the effort to approach the matter of means solely through the principle of proportionality is highly problematic. The concept is relatively new to moral debate, having come into use only over the last forty years, after being introduced by Ramsey in two books in the 1960s. The older just war tradition uses the approach found in the law of armed conflicts: some means are defined as not allowable, others as allowable. In practice, appeals to proportionality alone often do not involve calculations of proportionality—costs against effects—at all, but label any means of great destructive power "disproportionate." That is, the appeal to proportionality is prone to misuse. A further practical problem is that it establishes no bright-line criteria for determining whether a particular means may be used in a combat situation. The approach found in the older moral tradition and in the law of armed conflicts, by contrast, sets up such a bright-line distinction and provides a clear reference point for distinguishing allowed from forbidden means. Using calculations of proportionality within this framework as an aid to deciding among alternative allowed means is a way of further fine-tuning the actual choices. But forbidden means always remain forbidden.

The remaining type of bombing introduced in the newspaper excerpts above is bombing aimed at targets of a "dual-use" nature, that is, targets that have both military and civilian uses. Insofar as they are military, they may be directly, intentionally made the object of an armed strike; insofar as they are civilian, direct, intentional attacks are to be avoided, although collateral destruction is allowed under the principle of double effect. Legally, that is, they are permissible targets; morally, they are also permissible, although the noncombatant harm of the attack must be further justified by appeal to double-effect reasoning.

Double-effect reasoning addresses the problem of whether a given use of force is discriminate by distinguishing between its direct, intended effects and the indirect, formally unintended effects. If the good effects are direct and intended, while the bad effects are indirect and unintended, then the action is morally permissible. There remains to be considered, though, the balance between the good and evil effects, and this is where considerations of proportionality come into the picture. If a given attack on a dual-use target produces effects in which the destruction of military capacity is greatly outweighed by the harm done to noncombatants, then there is good reason to judge the targeting wrong as disproportionate. How this judgment should go, however, is often controverted. An example is the use of air strikes against the Iraqi electric power grid during the Gulf War of 1991. This was a dual-use target, inasmuch as both the Iraqi military and the civilian infrastructure depended on the electric power supplied by the grid. But destroying it had only a temporary effect on the Iraqi military capacity since the military had backup generating power and the manpower to put it in operation, while on the civilian side, loss of electric power disrupted the water supply, sewage disposal, and many aspects of everyday life until well after the cease-fire was signed. The destruction of the power grid has since been widely criticized as a bad decision, one that caused disproportionate harm to the civilians who depended on it, while conferring only limited and temporary military advantage. Whatever judgment one may reach on this, as a matter of fact, the power grid as such was not targeted by the air strikes of Operation Iraqi Freedom.

In the case of the bombing attack reported on March 27, the target was the Iraqi Ministry of Information complex. The military purpose was "to destroy the Iraqi government's ability to send orders to commanders and troops in the field." More generally, destroying the ministry complex was part of a larger aim of destroying elements of the Saddam Hussein regime, thus weakening it; in the words of Gen. Richard E. Myers, chairman of the Joint Chiefs of Staff, this was an example of "concentrating on regime command and control targets, and other targets that allow them to communicate either propaganda or with their military." At the same time, the complex provided civilian television service. In this case, the latter was temporarily disrupted, although mobile dishes quickly restored service. Even had the television service been disrupted for a longer time or permanently, this would not have been of the same order as the harm caused by interruption of the water supply and sewage disposal due to the 1991 strikes on the power grid. As for the announced military purpose, the Iraqi military also had backup communications equipment, but the disruption of the central command-and-control function of the ministry was significant. This was a case, in short, where the proportionality argument comes out favoring the strike against this dual-use target.

The destruction caused by bombing, then, is not all the same, considered either morally or legally. These three cases from the same day of the war illustrate the important differences made by the nature of the target, whether it was struck intentionally and directly, and whether the collateral effects outweigh the intended effects.


## WHAT CONSTITUTES A JUST WAR?

> *The Star-Ledger* (Newark, New Jersey), March 29, 2003, 1:
> Headline: "Iraqis Shell Citizens as They Flee Basra; Mortars and Machine-gun Fire Force Group of 1,000 to Turn Back"
> Headline: "In the U.S., a Just War. Around the World, a Different View"

In just war reasoning, the justice of the decision to resort to armed force is distinct from the justice of how justified armed force is used. A just war in the former sense may be unjustly carried out; conversely, a war undertaken unjustly may be carried out justly. This distinction is not always honored in debate about the matter of the justice of any particular armed conflict. In the stories under the two headlines above, the focus is on war conduct. The first of the stories focuses on Iraqi irregulars' firing on noncombatants as an example of wrongful conduct in war. The second of the stories, by contrast, describes how, in media accounts critical of the justice of the use of force by the United States and Britain, images of death and destruction were laid at the feet of the coalition, with no distinction as to immediate responsibility for the scenes used by these media. These two stories thus exemplify two quite opposite ways of thinking about harm done in the midst of armed conflict. The former reflects the way of thinking found in the just war tradition and the international law on armed conflicts: whatever the justice of the war in question, all parties are obligated to observe the justified moral and legal limits; if they do not, then they may be held to account for violating those limits. The media accounts depicted in the latter story reflect the way of thinking that holds the party who fires the first shot guilty for all the harm done in the war, whatever its nature and whoever its victims. So, apart from the debate over the resort to armed force in the first place, which is discussed in chapter 2, there is an ongoing debate throughout a conflict once it has begun that pivots on these two ways of thinking about the harm done during the conflict. For people taking the former view—which, as I have said, is that of the historical just war tradition and the law of armed conflicts—it matters critically whether a participant in the conflict observes the specified restraints in dealing with the enemy. For people taking the latter view, everything done in the conflict is judged in terms of their earlier judgment as to whose fault the war is. That is, these latter people project forward into the conflict their earlier arguments and judgments about the rightness of the resort to armed force. The first view seeks to impose restraints on the conduct of the conflict so as to spare noncombatants and limit overall destruction; the latter view has no purchase on limiting the conduct of the parties to the conflict because in its proponents' judgment the overriding moral question is who is at fault for the specific armed conflict.

Clearly, I am of the first view. The problem with the second is not simply or mainly that it confuses two distinct moral questions and ignores the content of the just war tradition, the historical "laws and customs of war," and positive international law. The critical problem is that it provides no purchase on limiting the conduct of parties to an armed conflict once it has begun. Indeed, the problem may go further: if one side is judged to be at fault in the first place, then the other side is regarded as the one fighting rightly. Anything the first side does is wrong, and correspondingly, the side that is in the right may do whatever it believes necessary to win. This view, then, is a recipe for unrestrained warfare. It is the wrong way to think about war, both at the beginning, in terms of its confused moral logic and ignoring of the law of armed conflicts, and at the end, in terms of its implications for all-out war.

## SUICIDE BOMBING

*New York Times*, March 31, 2003, A1:

A crude sign now stands at the checkpoint here where four Americans died when a bomb in a taxi exploded on Saturday. "Roadblock ahead," it reads, in Arabic. "Leave the area or we will fire."

The conventions of restraint in war are double-edged. On the one hand, they reflect the moral values of the culture out of which the soldiers come and which they are fighting to defend. This is what is signaled by the story above of the soldier who responded, "That's not who we are," to a question about whether the use of immoral and illegal tactics by Iraqi irregulars would lead the American army to act in kind. In practice, however, maintaining the conventions of restraint depends on certain assumptions about the enemy. The tactic of suicide bombing radically calls those assumptions into question. It is not simply that reciprocity is assumed, so that the enemy must show that he, too, is committed to observing the established restraints; when reciprocity is violated, there are practical means to take to try to restore it. More fundamentally, the practice of suicide bombing violates a deeper assumption about the enemy: that he too values human life, does not want to take it if he can avoid it, and recognizes that there are some who should be protected even in war. The history of people who have given their own lives for a larger cause—sacrificing themselves for their unit, their country, the values they stand for—is a long one, but the history and normative traditions of warfare—in Islamic culture as well as in the West—have always understood these self-sacrificial acts to be exceptional, never the rule. The use of suicide bombing as a tactic, to be repeated whenever those who orchestrate the bombings wish and are able to do so, changes the face of war in fundamental ways. The soldier who is the potential target of a suicide bomber or those whom that soldier is duty-bound to try to protect may no longer assume that the suicide bomber cares about taking human life at all, except in so far as doing so contributes to the cause the bomber serves. One effect is to radicalize the response: to open fire on any vehicle or person who enters a danger zone, no matter how innocent he or she may appear, no matter that the person is not given an opportunity to express his or her reasons for being there. The experience of a suicide bomber in a civilian taxi, as the story above illustrates, had the immediate effect of turning checkpoints into free-fire zones. One may regret this implicit erosion of the commitment to maintain noncombatant immunity, but it is entirely understandable and was foreseen by the planners who send suicide bombers into such places. But again, a deeper issue is what this does to the assumption about common humanity between the warring parties: if the enemy shows, by the practice of suicide bombing, that he regards his own life as an instrument and no more, then how do we treat him as one having a common humanity? It is important to say that one must, in response to such acts, still try to be faithful to one's own values, to say about the suicide bombers, "That's not who we are." Still, there remains the dehumanizing effect of a suicide bomber's action: denying a common humanity by denying his own humanity and that of those whom he has indiscriminately killed. Restraint in war requires valuing human life. Suicide bombing repudiates such valuing.

## SIEGE WARFARE

> *New York Times*, April 3, 2003, A1:
> Headline: "Goal of U.S.: Avoid a Siege"

There is something about the idea of siege warfare that reeks of ages past: medieval armies drawn up in camps surrounding a keep enclosing not only the defending forces but also all of the common people of the area, who have sought refuge inside the castle walls. Successfully taking such a stronghold puts enormous strains on even the best intentions to avoid harm to noncombatants and to avoid disproportionate destruction. It was in the context of siege warfare that the classic just war discussions of double-effect developed since in siege warfare, combatants and noncombatants were normally mixed up, while in a battle in the field, armies of combatants opposed each other. It was also in the context of thinking about siege warfare that one of the oldest efforts to ban a weapon as *mala in se* was put into words: the 1139 banning of siege weapons by the Second Lateran Council. No reasons for this ban were provided at the time, but such weapons, as they existed at the time, tended to cause damage both indiscriminate and disproportionate, and indeed, this was part of their design.

How, in practical terms, to make war on the combatant defenders, while sparing, so far as possible, the noncombatants in the besieged place, has continued to be the special moral problem attaching to siege warfare. For although there is next to nothing about it in recent moral reflection on war, and although the law of armed conflicts treats the case of sieges only indirectly, siege warfare is not simply a form of war found in the past. The American Civil War saw such major sieges as those of Corinth and Vicksburg, Mississippi, and the lengthy and destructive siege of Richmond, Virginia. The Franco-Prussian War saw Paris besieged and bombarded. World War II included the long, cruel sieges of Leningrad and Stalingrad. In the wars of the breakup of Yugoslavia, the ancient city of Dubrovnik was besieged and bombarded during the Croatian war for independence, Sarajevo was besieged throughout much of the Bosnian war, and the eastern Bosnian cities of Srebrenica, Zepa, and Gorazde were besieged, then stormed by force, with the women and children expelled as refugees and the men and boys of military age taken prisoner and killed. Siege warfare is a contemporary reality, as well as one from the past. Because of the mixture of combatant defenders and noncombatants of various sorts, sieges present an exceptionally messy problem for moral conduct in war.

In his brief discussion of siege warfare in *Just and Unjust Wars*, Michael Walzer cites Maimonides on the Talmudic law of sieges, which called for surrounding a city under siege on only three sides, leaving the fourth open so that those who would flee could do so. The influential nineteenth-century military theorist Henri de Jomini offered a similar prescription for conducting sieges, and this model was followed in the U.S. Army's siege of Corinth, Mississippi, during the Civil War. But the practical problems of this way of carrying out a siege are obvious. First, the opening that allows noncombatants to flee also allows supplies and relieving forces to come in, bolstering the defense. Second, that same opening may be used by the defending forces to escape (as happened at Corinth), so that they can fight on in another place.

The moral problems arise from the complex character of city life and the reasons for various sorts of people to be there during a siege. In the deep just war tradition on noncombatant immunity, one of the earliest developments was to add "and their lands and property" or some similar phrase to the lists of people normally not to be attacked in war. Since noncombatants depended on these lands and properties for their day-to-day lives, attacking, destroying, or confiscating them represented an attack on the lives of the noncombatants themselves. By contrast to a purpose-built fortification, a city or town is about providing the stuff of ordinary life. Making it a defended place does not change this. Nor does it change the fact that the majority of the people present are most likely not combatants. Civilians may be in a city or town under siege for various reasons: they may live there, have gone there voluntarily as refugees from fighting elsewhere, have been herded there by either the attackers or the defenders, or have chosen to go there to help with the defense. Only these last are combatants; the rest are noncombatants and worthy of being treated as such. Leaving an escape route open may not help, as the defenders may forcibly prevent the general population from leaving in the hope that their presence will prevent or dull the siege. Even when it is possible to leave voluntarily, some may choose to stay to keep an eye on their property, others may fear leaving or have no other place to go, and some may be physically unable to leave. All of them are at placed at risk by a siege or an attack, and even if the besiegers or attackers are committed to avoiding direct harm to noncombatants, it is the nature of such fighting that many of these people will be wounded or killed and their property damaged or destroyed.

An attacking force thus has many good reasons not to want to be drawn into besieging a city or town or having to fight the defenders in the streets, houses, and public building of the place. In addition to concern not to devastate the lives and property of the noncombatants there, such fighting is inherently risky for an attacking force because many of the defenders will be in civilian clothing, thus indistinguishable from noncombatants until they begin firing. Also, virtually all of the places from which defenders can fight—houses of worship, schools, private homes, stores, workshops and factories, public buildings—are normally off limits for direct targeting.

It is in fact the defenders who, by their choice to use the city or town in question as their base for operations, as a storage area for weapons and munitions, as a fortified place to impede the enemy, or all the above, make that city or town, all the civilian buildings there, and all the people inside it subject to harm. The defenders' choice to fight there is morally similar to the kind of case discussed earlier, in which irregular fighters use noncombatants as shields, pretend to be noncombatants themselves, and use noncombatants' structures and vehicles to gain military advantage.

All of this describes the sort of case U.S. forces expected if Saddam Hussein's forces decided to use the city of Baghdad as a place to make a last stand. On the one hand, there was fear that such fighting would lead to heavy casualties among the U.S. forces. On the other hand, there was the realization that noncombatant life in the city would inevitably be heavily harmed, perhaps devastated, as well. Both were very good reasons not to want to become involved in a siege.

No siege developed in Baghdad, but the more recent case of Fallujah shows what a battle for Baghdad might have looked like.

## THE MEANING OF VICTORY

*New York Times*, April 6, 2003, A1:
Headline: "Allies' New Test: How to Define Victory"

*New York Times*, April 15, 2003, A1:
Headline: "Pentagon Asserts the Main Fighting Is Finished
in Iraq"

These two headlines, separated by only little more than a week, illustrate the particular messiness of this conflict. The twin goals of the United States and its allies had been to remove Saddam Hussein and his regime, defeating the regime's military forces as a means to this end, and to follow that with the establishment of a free, democratic Iraqi government. By April 6, Saddam Hussein was on the run and his regime had lost effective control of the Iraqi state and its military. By April 15, the remaining major military units had been crushed, had melted away, or had surrendered. But some time would yet be needed before a new democratic government could be created, and in the meantime, the victorious military forces would have to become the makers and keepers of the peace, sources of sustenance for the population, and participants in the effort to repair and rebuild the society. From the perspective of the just war tradition, a use of armed force is not just unless it aims at peace, and I have argued above that this implies serious efforts to anticipate what establishing peace will mean after the conflict is over. While the military victory obtained in Operation Iraqi Freedom was amazingly rapid and astonishingly low in its destruction of lives and property, establishing and maintaining the peace since the end of "the main fighting" has proven much more difficult. The Bush administration has since been severely criticized for not having been sufficiently prepared for what it would need to secure the peace and to create the conditions for the free, democratically governed society it hoped to establish. While I think the record is not at all as bleak as the most vocal critics have held, I think that a particular legacy of the prewar debate was an insufficiency of resources for creating postwar peace. As I argued earlier, establishing peace in a war-torn society is far from easy, can be expected to take quite some time, and may involve continuing, low-level, but deadly, uses of armed force. Establishing peace in a society that has been systematically oppressed for a generation or more means it is likely that fundamental attitudes, expectations, relationship patterns, and even intellectual ability will need time to develop. Above, I suggested that the experience of peacekeeping and rebuilding in Bosnia and Kosovo provides about the best example of what is needed, the resources necessary, and how long it may take to reach the desired result. Two major factors present in these cases were not present in Iraq after Operation Iraqi Freedom, and the reason lies in the debate that preceded this use of armed force. These factors were broad international participation in the peacekeeping and rebuilding effort, shown through the commitment of personnel, policy support for the efforts, and funding to underwrite them, and the presence of a military force that could not be challenged by the forces of disorder. As to the first, I have said earlier that I believe the use of force to remove the Saddam Hussein regime was justified and that there are times when doing the right thing means acting alone or with a limited number of friends. But that also means that the nations that take such action are committed to securing the peace since those who opposed the action in the first place can hardly be expected—or trusted—to help afterward. In this regard, I am happy that early planning to withdraw U.S. and other coalition forces soon after the military victory was not carried through, for our obligation to the Iraqi people and Iraqi society continued after the military victory. Still, if Bosnia and Kosovo are useful guides, this means that very useful help is not available. The second factor is the size of the forces available to keep order. This conflict showed that it is possible for a relatively small, but well-equipped, highly trained, coherent, disciplined professional force to win a shooting war quickly and at relatively low cost. But this same force has had difficulty from the first in establishing and maintaining order. I am among those who think this is because they are simply too few in number. Again, the counterexample of the stabilizing forces in Bosnia and Kosovo suggests what is needed to succeed.

The obligation to Iraq now is to do the best possible with what is available. The obligation for the future is to make plans to deal better with such obligations should they arise again.

# THE WAR TO OUST SADDAM HUSSEIN: AFTER

# 5

# LOOKING BACK AS A WAY OF LOOKING AHEAD

The war to remove Saddam Hussein offers important lessons for future thinking about the use of armed force in all those contexts where such thinking goes on: the spheres of public policy debate and formulation, the military, international law, moral debate, and not least, the sphere of public understanding, considered generally. While this chapter touches on several of these contexts, it focuses on one of them, the moral debate, and looks specifically at the question of the moral use of armed force in terms of the perspective based in the classic just war tradition, which I have employed above in discussing Operation Iraqi Freedom and the debate that preceded it. I will treat six questions, some of them previously regarded as substantially settled but reopened as a result of this conflict, and others that have been newly raised by this conflict or by the larger context of the war against terrorism within which it is situated. The six questions are as follows:

- What should be the standard for preemptive use of military force?
- Is the idea of humanitarian intervention now dead?
- Is there a "world order" any more? What should the relationship be between states and the United Nations? What is the proper way to think about international law?
- What does this conflict mean for the future of war conduct? In particular, what effect does the threat posed by terrorism and by the practices of the Iraqi fedayeen and the postconflict insurgents have on the effort to protect noncombatants in armed conflict?
- What does it mean that a justified war should aim at peace? How should

postconflict "peace" be assessed? What obligations does the aim of establishing or restoring peace impose, and how far do they extend?
- What does this conflict imply for relations with the Islamic world and the war against radical Islamist terrorism?

## WHAT SHOULD BE THE STANDARD FOR PREEMPTIVE USE OF MILITARY FORCE?

As we saw earlier, the public debate of 2002–2003 over using military force against the Saddam Hussein regime quickly became, effectively, a debate over one of the three justifications offered by President Bush for the use of such force: the need to preempt the possible use of weapons of mass destruction (WMD) held by Iraq—either by Iraq itself or, more probably, by al Qaeda operatives, who would use them in a strike against the continental United States. The argument over this justification emerged again to dominate the debate over the war in the postconflict period, where the critical questions were whether Iraq under Saddam Hussein actually possessed WMD, and if it did, whether it also had ties to al Qaeda close enough that it would have furnished al Qaeda operatives with such weapons. Before the war, though, these questions were not the focal ones in the debate: the intelligence consensus, in other countries as well as in the United States, was that Iraq in fact possessed chemical and biological weapons, was actively engaged in developing a nuclear-weapons capacity, and was close to doing so. Since Saddam Hussein's Iraq was giving financial support to terrorist groups and providing asylum to wanted terrorists, it was easy to accept the likelihood of a link to al Qaeda. The focus in the debate over whether to use force in the first place was the question of preemption itself. Preemption was questioned on two levels: should it ever be allowed, and, if yes, what should be the standard for it?

Much of the context for the discussion of the first question was provided by the development of positive international law during the twentieth century, which itself was influenced by the destruction and loss of life of the two world wars. First came the Covenant of the League of Nations, following World War I, by which the parties to the covenant agreed to submit disputes to arbitration and not to resort to force to settle them, unless the arbitration had failed and a significant national interest was at stake. This was followed by the Pact of Paris (Kellogg-Briand Pact) of 1928, sometimes called "the agreement to outlaw war," which strengthened the emphasis on arbitration as a means of settling international disputes by providing that its signatories would not initiate the use of force for the settlement of a dispute (although, as American secretary of state Frank Kellogg clarified in response to a query, the right to resort to force in self-defense remained unchanged). Since the nations that began World War II were among the signatories, it may be judged that this effort to prevent the outbreak of war by international agreement had failed. Yet, this approach was taken up and restated in Article 2 of the U.N. Charter, which pledges members of the United Nations to "refrain . . . from the threat or use of force against the territorial integrity or political independence of any state." At the same time, the 1928 agreement's unwritten acceptance of self-defense as customary law was spelled out in positive law in Article 51, with two important restrictions: individual or collective self-defense was allowed only against "armed attack" and only "until the Security Council has taken measures necessary to maintain international peace and security." The restriction of defense to response to "armed attack" contrasted markedly with the rights given to the Security Council in Articles 39 to 42 to determine the existence of a "threat or breach of the peace or act of aggression" and to respond by it by measures up to and including the use of "air, sea or land forces as may be necessary." That is, the Security Council might authorize force to thwart a threat to international peace and security, while individual states or groups of states could use force only in defense against armed attack. The provision that individual or collective self-defense was allowed only until the Security Council had acted changed the rules for self-defense in another way: the use of force in self-defense was allowed only as an interim measure, until the Security Council had acted. This clearly assumed that the Security Council would act; if it did not, though, the interim measure might become one of longer duration.

The language of the Charter restricting the right of states, acting individually or collectively, to resort to armed force had an important effect on the language of military policy and on that of moral discourse on war. As the Pact of Paris shows, the earlier assumption had been that states had the right to resort to force to settle disputes. In practice, powerful states had employed force to further national interests, including establishing friendly governments, creating favorable conditions for trade by their nationals, and gaining territorial concessions to support their interests. Article 2 of the Charter took away all these assumptions about the right to use armed force, leaving to states only the right to use such force in defense. Defense thus became the term of art for defining the purpose of military force (as in the shift within the U.S. Cabinet from the "War Department" to the "Department of Defense") and for the allowable justification for resort to military force. This usage is reflected in the conceptualization of the idea of just war as this idea was recovered for public debate from the work of Paul Ramsey through that of Michael Walzer to that of the U.S. Catholic bishops and beyond.

Central to this usage was the idea of just resort to force as reactive to a prior use of arms. Walzer termed his discussion of the right to resort to force the "theory of aggression," while the Catholic bishops in their 1993 statement restricted the use of force to correcting "aggression or massive violation of the basic rights of whole populations." This was in accord with the charter's limiting the resort to force to a response to armed attack. In this conception, responsive use of force might be justified or unjustified, depending on circumstances, but first use of force (except, as the Catholic bishops and others argued in the 1990s, resort to limited uses of force to correct egregious violations of basic human rights) could, for many commentators, only be wrong.

What, then, of the idea of preemption, the first use of force in response not to an actual armed attack but in response to preparations well under way to undertake such an attack, coupled with the settled intent to carry it out? Classic statements of the just war idea did not stigmatize first resort to force because their concern was with responding to injustice, however it might be manifest. They did not prioritize defense against armed attack, and certainly did not define just cause in terms of such self-defense, reflecting Augustine's conception of just war: a Christian might not use force in self-defense because Jesus had forbidden that in his admonition to respond to violence against oneself by turning the other cheek; yet, a Christian might justifiably use force to protect an innocent neighbor against harm. Augustine's aim was not, as Ramsey later saw clearly, to justify use of force to respond to prior use of force—one did not have to wait until the neighbor had been harmed to act—but to show how force might be morally justified to prevent the harm from being delivered. Use of force after the fact of harm was described differently, not as "defense" but as recovery of that which had been wrongly taken away or punishment of wrongdoing. From the perspective of classic statements of the just war idea, there was no question that one might justifiably use force to prevent an attack by a wrongdoer as well as to repair the injustice caused by such an attack or to punish the attacker.

Such also was the perspective that developed in customary international law during the modern period. Hugo Grotius argued in *De Jure Belli ac Pacis* that, of course, it was justified to use force to ward off a blow about to fall, although he cautioned against stretching this allowance to justify war for just any sort of reason. Although the term *preemption* did not appear until the twentieth century, this basic idea became standard within the "laws and customs of war" as they developed throughout the modern period. The model here, as in Augustine, was that of the upraised sword ready to fall, or in the case of states, the gathering of armies on or near the frontier and other clear preparations, coupled with a manifest intention to use them. After the signing of the Treaty of Westphalia, which defined sovereignty in terms of territorial integrity, the intention to project such gathering force across the borders of the threatened state became an important element in the determination of whether that state might strike first to prevent the imminent invasion.

Article 51 of the U.N. Charter, in allowing use of force in self-defense only "if an armed attack occurs," changed the rules. The question was, how far did it do so? International law does not boil down to the content of the positive law or "black-letter law" of treaties and other agreements, including the Charter of the United Nations. Its precise content also depends on the actual behavior of states, which collectively defines customary international law. States may, at the time a treaty or other agreement is signed or ratified, express formal reservations about one or more provisions of the agreement or may stipulate that they interpret one or more specific points in a certain way. Other reservations or interpretations may remain unstated but appear in the behavior of states. In the case of the Pact of Paris, the agreement's black-letter language rejecting resort to armed force in case of international disputes did not explicitly allow for self-defense, but after the matter was raised, it was clarified that the customary-law allowance of use of force in self-defense was not restricted. Nothing was said in the pact about the United States' claims to be able to employ force in the Western Hemisphere in accord with the Monroe Doctrine or about colonial powers' claims to be able to exercise force in respect to their colonies, but presumably these too remained unaffected. Similarly, after the signing of the Charter, the major powers continued to exercise the use of force for hegemonic purposes in their recognized spheres of interest. If such practices are looked at as evidence of what the customary law provides, then it turns out that the black-letter language of the Charter is not as restrictive as it appears.

A defining event in regard to the meaning of this language and the question of the preemptive use of force was the 1967 Middle East war, when, in anticipation of an attack whose preparations were well under way, Israel launched a preemptive air strike against the Egyptian and Syrian air forces while they were still on the ground but shortly before they were to take off for an attack on Israel. The Arab states cried foul; so did the French government of Charles de Gaulle, which cited the language of the Charter as outlawing all uses of force, except those in response to armed attack, and all first uses of force as aggression. According to this interpretation, the Israelis were not engaging in preemption but were guilty of aggression. The Israelis and their supporters, by contrast, argued that waiting for an attack that was sure and imminent would insure that Israel would suffer great devastation to its ability to defend itself. The argument for the Israeli first strike not only revived the customary-law concept of the right to use of armed force for preemption of an imminent attack (the upraised sword about to fall), but it also provided a revised definition of what would constitute a threat sufficient to warrant preemption: the impossibility of defense if Israel had waited until the Arab states had struck first.

In the context of nuclear-weapons strategy, a similar argument was being advanced in this same time period, both in the United States and in the Soviet Union, to justify a first nuclear strike in a case when an enemy strike was expected. Since nuclear missiles could not be defended against once launched, the only way to prevent the destruction they would cause would be to strike them first, destroying them while still in their silos. In the rarefied arena of strategic nuclear thought, preference for a first strike never became policy, losing out to the concept of mutual assured destruction as a way to prevent an enemy's resort to nuclear weapons; it was undermined still further by the prospect of a strategic missile defense held out by President Ronald Reagan during his second term. In the American moral debate, however, opposition to preemptive first use of nuclear weapons was subsumed to a general opposition to any "war-fighting" use of nuclear weapons and, in the case of the American Catholic bishops, by a general "presumption against war" to be overruled only exceptionally.

All of this provides a background for the discussion of preemptive use of force against the Saddam Hussein regime during the debates of 2002–2003. On the one hand, there was the acceptance of justified first use of force both in traditional just war thought and in customary international law. On the other, there was the language of Articles 2 and 51 of the U.N. Charter, the first providing that U.N. members "shall refrain . . . from the threat or use of force" and the second allowing use of force in self-defense only in response to an armed attack that is already under way. In the moral debate, the latter was strengthened by opposition to any and all use of force as unjustified, except in the most exceptional circumstances (the conception of just war based on the presumption against war idea), with these defined restrictively along the lines of the charter's definition of the right of self-defense as only allowed in response to armed attack, and then, only until the Security Council could act. This rolled opposition to the preemptive use of force together with opposition to the use of force in general, confusing the debate somewhat but effectively removing the possibility that those who held this position would find preemption justified in any case whatever.

Another element in the American debate over whether to use force preemptively against Saddam Hussein was the appearance, after that debate had already begun, of National Security Strategy (NSS) 2003, the first update of the national security strategy of the United States after the September 11, 2001, attacks. This document explicitly accepted preemptive use of force against efforts by enemies to acquire "dangerous technologies," that is, WMD or technologies for the production of such weapons. "As a matter of common sense and self-defense," the document stated, "America will act against such emerging threats before they can be fully formed." Opponents of the preemption argument saw NSS 2003 as another effort to make the case for preemptive use of force against Saddam Hussein's regime, but while this version of the NSS stated the position more explicitly, earlier versions of the NSS had also endorsed preemptive action. The function of the NSS statement is to provide a general overview of the parameters of strategic policy. The NSS does not explain exactly what this will mean in concrete terms for the use of military force; that is, the function of the national defense strategy (NDS), which is based on the NSS. The NDS, unlike the NSS, is held closely. My point is that the critics of the acceptance of preemption in NSS 2003 made too much of this in the context of the particular debate over use of preemptive force against Saddam Hussein and his regime. First, acceptance of preemption was not new; second, it implied nothing specifically about the use of preemptive force in any particular case. Yet, it did enunciate in general terms the argument the administration and its supporters were making for use of military force in the particular case at hand: that preemption was necessary against the threat of WMD.

In terms of international law, the argument for preemption served to invoke the allowance of use of force for self-defense in the U.N. Charter and in customary international law. The moral argument reflected this context as well. Lacking a smoking gun, a clear link between Saddam Hussein's government and an armed attack on the United States, either already accomplished or demonstrably imminent, supporters of preemptive use of force employed an argument that followed the same lines as the pro-Israeli argument of 1967 and that for a first nuclear strike from the same period: using WMD, whether chemical, biological, or nuclear, Iraq could kill many Americans and cause much devastation either by a direct attack or by an indirect attack through terrorists hostile to America. By the fall of 2002, supporters of a military strike argued, the only way to exercise self-defense against such a threat was to depose Saddam Hussein and his regime and then to find and destroy the WMD.

Now, in principle, the standard offered in this argument was not new: changed circumstances present different measures of threat. Just as the September 11 attacks had come out of the blue, so could an attack using Iraqi WMD, with much more devastating results. The WMD threat is qualitatively, as well as quantitatively, different from the upraised sword or even a mobilizing army or the sailing of a naval fleet. The potential destruction of these weapons, those manifesting the threat, is so great and so difficult to prevent once the use of them is under way that new emphasis shifts to the matter of whether there is intent to do us harm. In the terms of the older standards for preemption, using force in this case looked like prevention, not preemption, and preventive war was against both the moral tradition and international law. Thus, the U.S. Catholic bishops explicitly labeled the proposed use of force "preventive" rather than preemptive. They went on to reject, in any case, the removal of the Saddam Hussein government, accepting only an effort to change that government's behavior.

The 2002–2003 debate, because of its focus on the preemptive use of armed force, revealed two important things. First, despite the positive-law effort to rule out preemption by restricting use of force in self-defense to response to armed attack, the customary-law acceptance of preemption remained alive and well in U.S. (and British) interpretations of the rights of states. Second, the standards for preemptive use of force were shifting. Just as in 1967, Israel and its supporters argued that a state has a right to engage in a preemptive strike to avoid certain devastating harm to itself by enemy air power, in 2002–2003, those who supported the preemptive use of force against Saddam Hussein argued that mere possession of WMD or even advanced efforts to obtain such weapons could warrant preemptive military action because of the ease of using such weapons by stealth and the nature of the destruction they would cause. This, it seems to me, is the standard that must now be evaluated and applied in future debates over the preemptive use of force.

What should these developments imply for moral thinking about war from a just war perspective? As I have noted, some participants in the debate of 2002–2003 opposed all uses of armed force, so the question of preemption was already answered (negatively) for them. This was a pacifist position, not a just war one. Others were opposed to the preemptive use of force because no actual attack had occurred; this position reflected the charter's restriction of the right of states to resort to armed force to responses to armed attack. But the classic just war conception of just cause for resort to force is better rendered in international law by the broader understanding of the right of self-defense in customary law: both allow for the preemptive use of force against a certain and imminent threat. Similarly, in the moral terms of the just war tradition, there is no reason to privilege a second use of force over a first use: indeed, in some circumstances, the first use of force may be the best way to discharge the moral responsibility to protect and preserve order, justice, and peace, at which good politics should aim.

Even so, it must be said that deciding whether there is justification for the preemptive use of force in a given case may be, and in the nature of things, most likely will be, extraordinarily difficult. For that determination will rest on judgments about facts that the adversary will try to keep well hidden, such as the state of weapons-development programs, the kind of weaponry available for war, plans for the use of troops in the event of war, and so on. Efforts at deception may mislead intelligence gatherers and interpreters. Even more difficult is determining whether there is an intention to attack. Intentionality may be measured by past behavior and current statements and actions, but these are not sure guides as to whether there is in fact an intention to take the action against which preemptive force would be directed. In the case of a despotic regime, intentionality is even harder to get at since the despot will reserve decisions to himself and shield his thinking from even his closest advisers. The case for preemptive use of force to oust Saddam Hussein exhibits both of these kinds of difficulties: the prewar intelligence consensus that Iraq possessed chemical and biological weapons in operational form and was close to developing nuclear weapons turned out to be false, and efforts to penetrate Saddam Hussein's intentionality were blunted by the wall of security he had erected to protect himself.

The difficulty of judging whether preemptive use of force is justified does not mean that it is never allowable; rather, as I have already said, in some cases, preemption may be the most moral course, heading off a more devastating use of force or a highly destructive war. But the difficulty of the judgment on preemption means that this justification needs to be used with care, and in practice, it is best backed up by other lines of reasoning as well.

Of the three justifications put forward by President Bush for using armed force to remove Saddam Hussein and his regime, the one which received the most attention in the public debate, preemption, was in my judgment morally and politically the weakest. The other two—the legal justification and the human rights justification—were inherently stronger in substance and more demonstrable, but they were neglected in the public debate. Yet, the fact that they existed was important in that they backed up the prudential judgments that had to be made regarding preemption. Although, as we now know, the intelligence consensus on WMD was at fault, these other justifications remain unaffected. This is thus another reason why the debate should have given more attention to them and not focused so exclusively on the argument over preemption.

## IS THE IDEA OF HUMANITARIAN INTERVENTION NOW DEAD?

Just war reasoning tends to support the idea of intervention for humanitarian purposes. The classic tradition makes no distinction as to whether the person or people in sovereign authority may use force in response to a violation of the peace at home or abroad; rather, while the moral responsibilities of government have, first of all, to do with securing the just and peaceful order of the sovereign's own political community, they extend also to protecting the frame of orderly, just, and peaceful relations among political communities, for without this, the good of each individual community is at risk. While Ramsey and Walzer did not know the historical just war tradition on this, they both reflected the inner moral logic of this tradition in favoring intervention for humanitarian purposes. Ramsey was more expansive about this, arguing that a powerful state like the United States bore a large share of responsibility for an international order that protected human goods. Ramsey held this responsibility to exist despite the United Nations, which he regarded as politically imperfect and structurally and materially too weak to perform this task. Walzer's treatment of humanitarian intervention was also positive but more restricted: he could find no historical cases in which an interventionary use of armed force had been conducted entirely for humanitarian reasons without some admixture of national-interest purposes.

The U.S. Catholic bishops, when they first laid out their conception of just war in 1983 in *The Challenge of Peace*, focused on limiting the uses of military force and forbidding any use of nuclear weapons as immoral. While they included "to protect innocent life" and "to preserve the conditions necessary for decent human existence" among their list of just causes for use of military force, they did not follow this out into consideration of humanitarian intervention. In their 1993 statement, though, the bishops made the question of humanitarian intervention a focal concern, using the following language to describe the criterion of just cause for resort to force: "Force may be used only to correct a grave public evil, i.e., aggression or massive violation of the basic rights of whole populations." Although they continued to hold that just war thinking begins with "a strong presumption against the use of force," they quoted Pope John Paul II, saying that intervention to halt and correct egregious violations of basic human rights may be an "obligation," then followed this up with language of their own echoing this judgment and their own earlier statement on just cause.

Other just war–based moral reasoning from this period about when the use of force is justified treated humanitarian intervention positively, even when other reasons for resort to force were denied: thus, in a 1998 statement from the General Assembly of the Presbyterian Church, use of force to respond to great violations of human rights was authorized, provided that there were no national-interest reasons attached. This language was absurd on the face of it for a variety of reasons: it wrongly imposed the nonresistance standard for individual moral behavior on political communities, ignoring the responsibility of the leaders of such communities to care for their own people; it took the wrong lesson from Walzer's observation that he had not found any actual cases in which armed interventions did not include motives of interest among humanitarian motives; and it entirely misrepresented the meaning of just war reasoning. But the Presbyterian statement showed the positive attitude toward humanitarian intervention that had developed at this time even among people who otherwise used just war reasoning to argue for a functional pacifism.

The context that nourished the growth of attitudes favoring humanitarian intervention—even when other possible uses of military force were looked on without favor—was established broadly by the end of the cold war, the collapse of the Soviet Union, and a corresponding lowering of fears about nuclear war. More particularly, though, the context in which prohumanitarian interventionist sentiment grew was established by the conflicts in Somalia, Rwanda, Bosnia, and Kosovo, as well as several other local conflicts closely watched by the media, in which the fighting directly or indirectly created great humanitarian need. Opponents of war, including those who used just war arguments to make their case, had habitually cited the humanitarian need created by war as a reason for the United States not to use military force in crises. As late as 1991, this line of argument was employed by opponents of the use of military force to roll back the Iraqi occupation and annexation of Kuwait. The two American church statements I have mentioned were prominent examples of moral stances based on this line of argument, which resonated broadly within America's public tradition of being a "light to the nations," a powerful influence for good in the world. The altruism expressed here fit well also within a

Christian moral tradition that emphasized love for the needy neighbor, even at the price of self-sacrifice. The result was a way of thinking that was the polar opposite of reasoning that began with protection of interests: the prohumanitarian interventionism of the 1990s at its most extreme—as in the Presbyterian statement of 1998—was an expression of moral idealism that shared nothing with the politics of realism. In order for an interventionist use of force for humanitarian purposes to have nothing to do with national interest, or even to fly in the face of such interest, was from this perspective a strong plus, not a minus.

This fundamental opposition between two ways of thinking about how the United States should act in the world helps to explain, I think, why the argument for the use of force to depose Saddam Hussein because of his egregious violations of the human rights of Iraqis and Iraq's neighbors alike did not gain traction in the American debate during 2002–2003. The case against Saddam Hussein was strong: the use of chemical weapons against his own people and a neighboring state, his arbitrary imprisonment and mistreatment of dissidents, his use of sadistic torture against his enemies and their families, and his use of public funds to build palaces while the majority Shiite population of Iraq lacked medicine for their sick and food for their children. The use of armed force in Bosnia and Kosovo provided positive precedents, while recriminations over not using force to oppose and end the Rwandan genocide in 1994 bore the message that force is sometimes necessary to combat great evil and the threat of more evil. But these were all cases in which the idealistic reasons for acting dominated reasons based in national interest. The Iraq debate was different: the argument for preemption was a specific case of reasoning from the national interest. For those who favored use of military force for humanitarian purposes, while opposing the use of such force for the purposes of national interest, this tainted the humanitarian argument.

I have repeatedly said that the humanitarian argument for using force against Saddam Hussein was strong and should have been given more attention in the moral debate. That is because just war tradition does not make moral idealism the opposite of national interests. Rather, both are included in the conception of what political responsibility requires. For people in positions of sovereign authority, protecting the common good of their own political community and the just and orderly peace of that community is their first duty. While it is important also to seek the good of those in other communities, it would be an abrogation of moral responsibility to their own people for leaders to seek the good of others without taking into account the good of their own. For this reason, if Walzer was surprised to find a mixture of interests and humanitarian motives in the historical cases of humanitarian intervention he identified, he should not have been; if he was bothered that there were no purely humanitarian motivations without any justifications based in interests of the intervener, he should not have been. Indeed, moral reasoning about the use of armed force within the tradition of just war needs to begin with such a mixture, reflecting concern both for one's own people, as well as for others whom the use of such force may seek to protect and vindicate.

This position will satisfy neither the realists, who hold that only reasons of national interest can justify use of armed force, nor their polar opposites, those who hold that use of force for national-interest reasons is inherently immoral and that only uses of force for purely altruistic humanitarian reasons is ever justified. In the case of the humanitarian argument for the use of force against Saddam Hussein, both of these groups opposed it for their own reasons.

But just war tradition requires that the possibility of using armed force to correct grave humanitarian wrongs should remain on the table. It should be clear that the issue here is not the use of military personnel and equipment to deliver aid in cases of natural disasters, such as the 2005 tsunami in the Indian Ocean, which is not controversial, but the use of military force to stop and correct serious and continuing violations of basic human rights and needs by people and groups who misuse their power, oppressing these people for their own selfish ends. This is what was at stake in the cases of Rwanda, Bosnia, and Kosovo, and it was also clearly at stake in the case of Iraq under Saddam Hussein. The standards applied in these earlier cases should also have been applied here. For an individual state or group of states to do this runs afoul of the U.N. Charter's prohibition against resort to force except in response to armed attack. This prohibition, in turn, rests on an understanding of sovereignty in terms of territorial borders, so the fundamental problem with using force across another state's borders is that it may violate the protections due to sovereignty. But in the case of a state's having already used force in an armed attack, those protections disappear, and the guilty state may be attacked in return. Understanding sovereignty in terms of the moral responsibility of a government to care for the common good of its own citizens and a just and peaceful international order sets up a different test for when the protections due sovereign status disappear.

When those in power within a political community use that power for the purpose of oppressing some or all their own people, they violate the fundamental responsibilities of sovereignty; they are tyrants, not sovereigns. And those who seek to follow out rightly the implications of the responsibilities of sovereignty have a right to seek to stop this oppression. Where the oppression extends to the violation of victims' basic human rights—including wrongful denial of food, medicine, and liberty, as well as explicit acts like arbitrary killing, imprisonment, and torture—there should be no question that the line has been crossed into tyranny and that other states may use force, if necessary, to end this tyrannical abuse of power. This does not, of course, mean that resort to force is the right thing in every given case; establishing the moral justification is not the same as establishing the wisdom or necessity of using force, here as in cases where the moral justifications are different. This is another reason why it is important to take into account the interests of one's own people and of the international order more generally, along with the plight of the victims of such fundamental oppressions.

## WHAT OUGHT WE TO LOOK FOR IN "WORLD ORDER"?

The debate over use of armed force against Saddam Hussein and his regime laid bare some fundamental differences between Europeans and Americans in their thinking about the United Nations and the role of individual states. I put the matter in these terms, and not in terms of differences between the specific policy positions taken by the United States and Britain in the Security Council and the positions of those European states, France and Germany, that took the lead in opposing the use of force in this case. While there were (and are) such policy differences between the opposing powers and different perceptions of national interest, there were also more fundamental differences in how the opponents in this debate represented the role of the United Nations, the rights of individual states, and the nature of international law.

The difference over international law is fundamental. The continental European understanding of law is rooted in the positive-law tradition, according to which law is promulgated from the top down, and this imposes a duty to obey. The American and British understanding of law, by contrast, comes out of the common-law tradition, by which law is generated from the bottom up, from the accepted views and practices found in the society. In this view, law crystallizes around what is commonly held to be right. Of course, there are positive-law elements to the conception of law in the United States and Britain, but more importantly, the common-law approach is lacking in the continental European understanding of law. When these different conceptions of law are applied to the understanding of international law, the result is that continental Europeans default to a positive-law conception, while American and British interpreters make more of the practice of states, reflected in their understanding of customary international law.

Where authority to resort to force is concerned, the continental European view emphasizes the role of the United Nations as a kind of supersovereign entity, privileges the strong prohibition against the resort to force by states in Article 2 and the conditional character of the statement of the right of self-defense in Article 51, and reserves to the collective action of the Security Council any decision to use force to respond to threats to international peace and order, as provided in Articles 39 and 42. In this view, states have ceded the right to determine for themselves when they may employ force, and the black-letter law of the Charter now imposes this as a duty. In the United States and Britain, by contrast, the common-law tradition influences the interpretation of what actually is the content of international law, including the status of the United Nations as an organization and the black-letter provisions of the Charter. From this perspective, things often look very different. The behavior of states, especially major states, influences and conditions what the black-letter law means. The United Nations is viewed as an organization of states that retain their sovereignty, not as a supersovereign entity whose authority surpasses that of states, and the charter's treatment of the right of states to resort to armed force in Article 2 and Chapter VII (which includes Articles 39, 42, and 51) is understood through the prism of the sovereign state's right to protect its vital interests.

Thus, while European commentators have focused on the charter's restriction on the first resort to force and the need for a Security Council resolution to authorize use of force by any state, commentators in the United States—not least, people expressing official government policy, but certainly not them alone—have insisted that the Charter does not take away the right of national self-defense and that the concept of preemption, although one involving first use of force, must take into account the realities of contemporary terrorism and the possibilities of a devastating sneak attack using WMD. If terrorists and rogue states could be counted on to obey the positive-law prohibition against an attack and to abide by the outlawing of WMD in the positive law, then targeted states would be in a different relation to that law, but that is not the world as it is. Thus, the limits on use of force in the positive law cannot be the last word: threatened states have the right to use force to prevent such an attack or to respond to one.

My views on the United Nations as an organization were first expressed in the context of the debate over military intervention to end egregious abuses of human rights in my 1999 book *Morality and Contemporary Warfare*. In sum, these views are as follows: The United Nations lacks the attributes of sovereignty; it is not a superstate sovereign entity but a cooperative organization of sovereign states. It lacks responsibility and accountability to the people of the world whom it professes to represent, for only its member states can hold it responsible for its actions. Where use of force is concerned, its lack of sovereignty is also expressed in the fact that it has no military forces of its own and only a very limited and inadequate command-and-control capability for those forces that operate on its behalf. Thus, it cannot responsibly direct them. It provides a framework for cooperative action by states, but when this breaks down or becomes paralyzed for whatever reason, it is the states that, because of the responsibilities inherent in the idea of sovereignty, bear the responsibility for action and may act in the face of pressing need. It is good that there be some consensus and some degree of common participation in needed action because this provides an inherent check on the particular views and self-interests of any particular state; yet, while this consensus and common participation may be pursued within the context of the United Nations, it is not limited to that context. The purpose of the United Nations is to serve the goal of a peaceful and just world order, but states have responsibilities of their own in pursuing this goal, and the existence of the United Nations does not take away those responsibilities.

The conception of world order, what it requires, and who is responsible for establishing and maintaining it means different things to different people today. In 1990–1991, justifying the use of armed force to drive the occupying Iraqi army out of Kuwait and roll back Iraq's annexation of Kuwait, President George H. W. Bush repeatedly characterized this as an action in support of "world order." The justification of that use of force was clearly in accord with the black letter of positive international law, as well as with the customary law: it was an action of collective self-defense in response to an overt and incontrovertible act of first use of force against Kuwait. Even without Security Council approval, the coalition formed to respond to this aggression had the right of self-defense as spelled out in Article 51 of the Charter and in the customary-law understanding of self-defense. But the Security Council also gave its mandate for this action. The concept of world order and its relation to international law and to both individual states and the U.N. organization was more consensual and clear in this case than it had been for many decades, perhaps since the founding of the United Nations in 1945. Even so, some of the same people and groups who later opposed the use of force in 2002–2003 did so in 1990–1991, despite this clear authorization and justification in terms of world order. In the debates of 2002–2003, there was no consensus as to what maintaining world order required, and the Security Council's members differed on the matter of justification and authorization for force. The rather minimal resolution the Security Council managed to produce after much negotiation, Resolution 1441, was interpreted differently by those favoring force, on the one hand, and those opposing it, on the other. In this context, it was much less convincing than it had been in 1990–1991 to argue for a conception of world order centered on the existence of the United Nations as an organization. What remained were diverse conceptions of world order assumed by the various factions in the debate and outside it.

Besides the differences between the United States and its supporters, on the one hand, and France, Germany, and their supporters on the other, there was a third conception of world order very much in evidence but not addressed in the Security Council debate: the conception of world order advanced by the radical Islamists, who looked to the use of force against America and the West as a way to establish a new caliphate and a worldwide Islamic state. In this conception, both the United Nations and individual states not ruled by radical Islamist governments are illegitimate and must be destroyed in the effort to establish the genuine world order of a universal *dar al-islam*. So, by contrast with the case of 1990–1991, three major conceptions of world order compete today: one focused on the U.N. organization as a kind of supersovereign entity, one focused on the goal of a universal Islamic state, and one focused on the responsibilities of states both to combat evil where it exists and to foster the sorts of conditions in other states—freedom, equality, and democratic self-rule—conducive to justice and peace within all states and in the relations of states with one another.

What does the idea of just war imply with regard to these three conceptions? The key lies in the just war tradition's roots in the classic Augustinian understanding of politics and the grounding of that understanding in Augustine's theology of history as laid out in *City of God*. Augustine saw history as in the process of gradually being transformed by grace, symbolized in his conception of the "city of earth," ruled by *cupiditas* (sinful love), as being remade into the "city of God," a society characterized by *caritas*, or orientation toward God in everything. The completion of this transformation will come only at the end of history; during history, life in society is characterized by a mixture of these two loves.

This conception has some similarities to the classic Islamic understanding of history as being transformed from the territory of war (*dar al-harb*) into the territory of submission to God (the *dar al-islam*), the understanding used by radical Islamists to define their own view of the ideal world order. Fundamentally, however, these conceptions are different. Augustine was describing the work of God, remaking sinful humankind by the infusion of a love that originated with him and entered the world through the self-giving sacrifice of Christ, and the city of God is not a goal for historical human striving but an ideal that stands outside of history. The making of a worldwide dar al-islam, by contrast, is to be a human achievement, the extension of rule according to Muslim law (sharia), understood as given by God, over the world as a whole, and this is to be accomplished within history. Armed force, in the form of the jihad of the sword, plays an important part in this achievement, imposing submission to God's law on those who refuse to submit voluntarily. This is a religiously described conception of a utopian social and political ideal to be brought about in history by the righteous.

By contrast, the Augustinian city of God is an ideal conceived as already present and at work, although not fully realized, throughout history. In this conception, the ends of good politics are known and are the same throughout history, the same for the city of earth, the city of God, and every form of human society in between. It is not the ends that are different—a just and peaceful social and political order—but the ability to achieve them. While human political communities in history are never able fully to achieve these goods, they can recognize them and understand their meaning, and it is their moral responsibility to seek to bring them into being so far as possible. Here, the justified use of force (*justum bellum*, or "just war") aims at defending against challenges to this effort, restoring the good where it has been impaired, and punishing those who do evil in opposition to the effort to do good. Justified use of force is a tool for the discharge of political responsibility—responsibility for the common good and to create or maintain a just and peaceful order within the political community.

While this conception establishes a powerful moral understanding of the state, it does not have anything to say directly about whether there might be a single world order in which a single sovereign authority might exercise responsibility for justice, order, and peace throughout the world. Indeed, the roots of the modern world-order movement lie in the Enlightenment-era effort to achieve "perpetual peace" through establishing a new political order superior to existing states, which would adjudicate disputes and thus maintain peace. But the most effective criticism of the idea of world order as requiring the institutionalization of such a superstate has always been that there simply is not such a superstate, that the United Nations in particular does not constitute one, and that in the world as it is, political responsibility for achieving a just and peaceful order lies with particular political communities, that is, with individual states. These ought to seek to work together for the good of all, just as individuals in their social relations ought to cooperate for the common good, but the responsibility to do so comes from within and does not require any superior authority to mandate it.

In the contemporary world, it may well be that the European Union is evolving in such a way that it will become a superstate, succeeding its constituent states in fundamental ways and thus altering the locus of responsibility for achieving the common good of a just and peaceful order among its members and in their relations with other political communities. But the European Union is not yet such a superstate; nor is the United Nations, on a global scale, either in theory or in performance. That leaves responsibility for defending the good to states, and practically speaking, because of its size, power, and global reach, the United States bears a heavier responsibility than others for doing this. Using its authority and its power, including military force, in the pursuit of a just and peaceful world order is, thus, not an exercise of national hubris but an expression of political responsibility. Other states have a similar responsibility, and this implies that the good of a just and peaceful world order should be a cooperative undertaking. But the locus of the moral responsibility still lies with each state.

## WHAT DOES THE EXPERIENCE OF THE WAR TO OUST SADDAM HUSSEIN MEAN FOR THE FUTURE CONDUCT OF WAR?

Two radically opposite ways of conducting war stand out from the war to oust Saddam Hussein and his regime, both sketched earlier in chapter 4: one is characterized by formal rules of engagement, target selection, weapons choice, soldier training, command decisions, and the individual decisions of soldiers aimed at fighting so as to avoid harm to noncombatants and to minimize destruction to Iraqi civilian life; the other is characterized by deliberate actions by Iraqi irregulars to endanger noncombatants in order to gain military advantage, to locate themselves among noncombatants so as to encourage destruction of noncombatant lives and property, and to pretend to be noncombatants so as to erase the combatant-noncombatant distinction in the minds of coalition soldiers. For some contemporary military commentators, these two opposite phenomena are linked in a destructive way: faced with overwhelming military power that they cannot defend against directly, an inferior enemy must resort to means that deliberately endanger noncombatants. When raised in the context of military discussions of contemporary armed conflict, this hypothesis aims at warning combatants that they cannot always expect the enemy to fight by the same rules they are seeking to follow and that, by confronting this likelihood in advance, they can be better prepared for how to deal with it within their own rules of engagement and their own moral self-understanding.

But another, somewhat darker, conclusion can be drawn from the suggestion that there is a link between the use of overwhelming force, even when applied with great care to observe established legal and moral restraints, and the enemy's resort to measures that ignore such restraints or use them for their own military advantage: that the relationship is one of cause and effect, that the use of overwhelming force itself causes the "dirty war" response. This way of thinking tends to absolve those who employ this response: they have been provoked into it, and the more fundamentally guilty are those who challenged them with overwhelming force in the first place. In the logic of this reasoning, the way to avoid the effect is to remove the cause. One way of following this out is to argue, as some do, that the principle of proportionality implies opposing force with force so as to have a "fair" fight. According to this reasoning, in such a conflict, presumably neither adversary would engage in tactics that violate noncombatancy for military advantage because both would understand that the contest is an even one and that they both may win without such tactics. In another context, I have observed that this reasoning is flawed in two fundamental ways, one having to do with the logic of the reasoning and the other having to do with the results. First, the principle of proportionality does not imply maintaining rough equality between the opposing forces, but it requires measuring the level and means of force to be used against the justified results desired. Second, in practice, use of overwhelming force can "blanket" an area of conflict so as to snuff out resistance, while use of lower levels of force can lead to a drawn-out, ultimately more destructive conflict. In my view, the tactically overwhelming force employed by the coalition in Operation Iraqi Freedom showed itself to be proportionate by its results, the quick collapse of the opposing forces, while the lack of a genuinely overwhelming force for establishing order and peace in Iraq after the overthrow of the Saddam Hussein regime illustrates the likely result of a disproportionately small application of force, a drawn-out, bloody conflict.

We must, however, question in additional ways the notion that the application of overwhelming force causes the use of means that violate established legal and moral constraints on conduct in war. First, there is no real evidence of a causative link; violation of noncombatant immunity has been a characteristic feature of much recent warfare, whether in cases in which the adversaries have roughly equal forces, such as Zaire/Congo, Sierra Leone, and Ivory Coast, or cases in which the worst offenders have superiority in the use of force, like the Rwandan massacre in 1994 and the Serb forces' behavior in Srebrenica late in the Bosnian war. Second, the intention to fight indiscriminately and preparation to do so may exist before the conflict actually begins, so the use of such methods is independent of the type or level of force used by the other side. We know this to have been the case with the Iraqi fedayeen and with preparations for a continuing war of insurgency. We know this to be the case in a different way for followers of al Qaeda, who wage war on noncombatants because of their ideology. That application of overwhelming force somehow causes the underdog to fight back by striking at noncombatants, using noncombatants for the underdog's own purposes, and trying to get the superior force to undermine itself morally by also resorting to such tactics—in short, the hypothesis that there is a cause-and-effect link between the two—simply does not stand up under even moderately close scrutiny.

This said, the problem remains: can conduct in war be successfully restrained, and if so, how? Again, the war to oust Saddam Hussein provides two very different perspectives on this question and how it may be answered. On the one hand, force was committed to fighting according to the established norms so as to respect noncombatant immunity and avoid disproportionate destruction; this is the first perspective, and the issue here is what this commitment implies for contemporary warfare. On the other hand, an opposing force, including irregulars, fought by directly, intentionally harming or endangering noncombatants to gain military advantage. This poses the issue in terms of violation of noncombatant immunity. The reasonable fear that the Iraqi forces might use chemical or biological weapons raised a further issue, that of proportionality as well as discrimination. In the face of such violations or threats of violation, two rather different questions must be addressed: how to respond to such violations when committed and how to get those fighting or about to fight in this way to respect the established limits.

In discussing Operation Iraqi Freedom above, I argued that the conduct of coalition forces set a new standard for conduct in major military operations. Several factors contributed to this, all important in various ways: the rules of engagement, which were extensive, yet well summarized for practical use by the troops, and which were conscientiously followed; the selection of targets for the air campaign, with particular sites marked off in advance as not to be struck and other targets identified and prioritized as to be targeted; care in the choice of weapons, angles of attack, and delivery vehicles both in the air campaign and on the ground; a structure for command decisions that incorporated legal advice at various levels to help deal with ambiguous cases, coupled with sophisticated communications that allowed the most difficult decisions to be made at the highest levels of command; a highly trained and disciplined force, whose training had included inculcation of values and attention to right behavior; individual decisions that reflected this training and discipline; and not least, but also not the most important, the availability of technology that allowed close and accurate targeting and choice of means to match the purpose of a specific action. While the sophisticated communications and precision-guided munitions (PGMs) used by the American forces received (and deserved) much attention in this conflict, they are far from the whole story. The presence of the other factors named show the intent to fight according to the established legal and moral restraints, as well as some of the results of carrying out this intention. But the availability and use of sophisticated new technology, including not only communications technology and PGMs but also the use of pilotless aircraft to observe the enemy closely and, in some cases, attack specific targets, elevated the carrying through of the intention to a level previously not attained and still not attainable by any other military, with the exception of the British military in some respects.

Most of the moral discussion of conduct in war takes as its model a situation in which the most important factors affecting such conduct are, first, the existence of legal and moral limits and, second, the obligation to observe these limits. I have been mostly alone in arguing that this obligation also requires taking concrete steps to structure one's military forces toward carrying out this obligation. That means discipline, training, inculcation of a moral sense, good rules of engagement, and careful attention to command and control, but it also implies the responsibility to develop weapons, strategies, and tactics oriented toward observing the established limits. Ramsey, in his moral treatment of nuclear weapons, reasoned similarly, arguing that only if nuclear weapons were used in a counterforce capacity could their use be moral. This followed from his commitment to the primacy of the principle of discrimination in his thought: only such targeting of nuclear weapons could clearly and certainly manifest the intention not to harm noncombatants directly and intentionally. I agree with this line of reasoning so far as it goes; it is vital to have plans for the use of existing weapons that are as faithful as possible to the legal and moral restraints on the conduct in war. But I think and have argued since I first began to write on morality and war that there is a further obligation to seek to develop weapons that are inherently more discriminating and less destructive.

One reason why earlier decades saw a race to produce ever-more destructive weaponry, from ever-heavier artillery to ever-larger bombs to ever-higher-yield nuclear and thermonuclear weapons, was that the ability to deliver them on target was technologically limited. The amount of destructive power needed to destroy or disable a particular legitimate target sets a standard for the weaponry used against it. If you cannot be sure of hitting the target with any one weapon, then you must use many, or you must increase the destructive power of each weapon so as to compensate for the known lack of accuracy of the delivery system. If the accuracy is increased, however, so that each weapon falls on its target, then the destructive force of that weapon can be decreased to the level needed to disable that particular target. Applied across the board, this leads to replacing nuclear weapons with conventional ones, to using smaller rather than larger bombs, to using relatively smaller warheads still in precision-guided missiles, and so on. Better communications and control technologies combine with advances in delivery systems to offer still another advantage, the ability to hit a desired target from a variety of angles so as to minimize collateral harm.

As I have noted above, for the particular case of the war to oust Saddam Hussein, much contemporary moral reflection on war still seems to assume that war inevitably means indiscriminate and disproportionate destruction on the model of the countercity bombing campaigns of World War II, with the possibility of escalation to the even greater destructiveness of nuclear weapons. Moralists need instead to take into account the new type of warfare made possible by increased targeting accuracy, better intelligence, and closer command and control, the downsizing of weapons, and the ability to strike targets in such a way as to minimize collateral damage. Change in this direction must not only be acknowledged but must also be supported and encouraged as morally right. We also need to reflect specifically on how to tailor the movement toward more discriminate and less destructive uses of military force in the future. Some commentators have already begun to argue that new weapons technology makes its use too easy for political decision makers. Instead of an expeditionary force, for example, one may instead launch a few cruise missiles. So far as this reasoning is correct, it suggests giving additional attention to the limits inherent in the moral restraints on resort to armed force; moralists belong in this debate alongside participants from the military and policy fields, but they must think in terms that accurately reflect what is possible in the use of armed force today. It might be argued that the dramatically increased ability to fight discriminately and less destructively should be shared with other states as a step in making war as a whole more discriminate and less destructive. While this would be an interesting idea, I think it is flawed. In the first place, the U.S. military bears the responsibility for remaining ahead of potential threats so as to be able to defend against them effectively, and technological superiority is one element in doing this. In the second place, so far as it may be correct that having such technology increases the likelihood of its use, expanding its availability would tend to make the world as a whole more dangerous. And third, in the quest to increase adherence to the established restraints on conduct in the use of armed force, there is still a great deal to be done independently of the question of the new military technologies.

This last point leads directly to consideration of the problem of fighters who ignore the established restraints or directly and intentionally violate them in the effort to gain military advantage. Earlier I raised two questions about this phenomenon: how the opposing side should respond to it and how to think about getting the violators to observe the restraints.

Answering the first of these questions is, in principle, easy: the opposing side should stick by its commitment to observe the established restraints. They should do this, most fundamentally, because of their moral commitment to these restraints; that is, they should observe them because violating them would go against who they are as moral beings. This answer in principle may go very far. In practical terms, however, some people may react in the way the violators want them to react: by engaging in indiscriminate, disproportionate conduct themselves. To counteract this tendency in advance is the work of military training, discipline, and socialization in the proper conduct expected of a soldier, but this must be reinforced by command behavior and decisions showing that the violation of these restraints is wrong, whichever side does it. Disciplinary action, up to and including legal prosecution, is the right response to violations already committed.

An argument in the other direction is provided by the principle of reciprocity in the customary law of armed conflicts. This provides that a violation of accepted conduct by one side may be met with a similar, although not necessarily identical, action by the other side to punish the initial violators and deter them from further violations. If the other side engages in abuse or torture of prisoners, for example, we may do so too or may take other action to punish and deter the enemy from continuing to treat prisoners in this way. While there is certainly a principle of reciprocity in the customary law and in the moral tradition it reflects, I am not convinced that it ever justifies actions that are wrong in themselves. To take the example just mentioned, the torture of prisoners is, I believe, always wrong, and the fact that my enemy is doing it does not excuse my doing it. Reciprocity rightly understood, I would argue, extends only to doing what is morally allowed. This implies that a response to an immoral or illegal action may involve applying force more stringently than would otherwise have been employed, but not engaging in the same behavior as the enemy. There are two fundamental problems in interpreting reciprocity to allow engaging in the same wrong behavior: it dehumanizes the people who carry out the wrong acts, and matching a violation with the same violation will likely lead to escalation. That is, this interpretation of reciprocity does not cause the enemy to leave off his bad behavior but reinforces it as he tries harder and harder to undermine his adversary's moral integrity.

Another problem with applying the principle of reciprocity in the wrong way is that the violator may simply not care about the victims of his conduct or their counterparts on his own side. That is, if an attack on the adversary's noncombatants were met by a reciprocal attack on their own noncombatants, those who carried out the first attack might not care; indeed, they might be delighted if their purpose was to get the adversary to violate his own moral code. In the case of the Iraqi fedayeen who used civilians as shields in fighting against the British forces in the battle for Basra or who actually fired on Iraqi civilians trying to escape the city, responding by attacking those same noncombatants would have been absurd as well as deeply wrong morally. Similarly, the fedayeen who disguised themselves as civilians to attack U.S. forces moving toward Baghdad would likely have been delighted this had led the U.S. forces to begin targeting Iraqi civilians indiscriminately.

Such behavior is not limited to these examples from Iraq; nor is it limited to the activities of terrorist groups. The intentional endangering of noncombatants and direct, intended attacks on noncombatants have been features of the actual face of war for the last half-century—local and regional armed conflicts, often driven by ethnic or ideological forces. Here, the enemy is demonized as "other," and the distinction made in the legal and moral definition of combatants and noncombatants—that the former take direct part in the military activities, while the latter do not—is rejected. Mere membership in the enemy group makes one a target. Moreover, members of the enemy group are often represented as less human or as otherwise deserving of death. Both underdogs and superior forces have made similar arguments and engaged in similar practices. Nor is the erosion or disappearance of respect for noncombatant immunity the only problem: once the enemy is demonized or dehumanized, it is possible to use otherwise stigmatized or banned weapons, such as chemical, biological, and radiological weapons. So far, the lack of resources of the adversaries in these local wars has largely limited their means to conventional weapons, like rifles, machine guns, and mortars (sometimes only knives, as in Rwanda in 1994), but the Iraqi use of chemical agents to suppress the Kurds and in the war with Iran shows us what might be should access to such weapons proliferate.

Can this trend toward observation of no limits in the conduct of war be reversed? If so, how? There is, unfortunately, no single answer. The 1977 Protocols to the 1949 Geneva Conventions attempted to address this problem, already abundantly manifest at that time, by explicitly extending the legal limits that had previously pertained only to war between and among states to noninternational armed conflicts—that is, conflicts in which one or more parties were not states. Although the protocols are flawed and in need of reformation in various ways, this was an important step in trying to establish that all armed conflict, whether international or noninternational in nature, is bound to observe the same fundamental restraints. Also, in the sphere of positive international law, the rise of human rights law since the Universal Declaration of Human Rights in 1948 has made explicit the fundamental values behind the protection of noncombatant immunity. So far, as the idea of even the most basic, universal human rights is accepted, representing the whole population of an adversary in armed conflict as "other," to be dehumanized or demonized, is recognized as wrong.

In the moral sphere, it is not only the just war tradition that mandates restraint in the use of armed force, protecting noncombatants, and prohibiting the use of indiscriminately and disproportionately destructive means; the moral traditions of other major cultures do so as well. Specifically for the case of the Iraqi fedayeen, the present-day Iraqi insurgency, and the terrorism of al Qaeda and its affiliates, the classic Islamic religious tradition defines limits on the prosecution of war, even when, as in the case of the jihad of the sword, that war is religiously justified and authorized. These limits are fundamentally similar to those found in the just war tradition and in the law of armed conflicts. Taking all of this together, there is a clear consensus that war on noncombatants and war involving indiscriminate and disproportionately harmful weapons is wrong. Realizing this is the first step toward stopping such practices in war. But it is not enough that the elements of this consensus are there; there must be a consistent effort to extend and enforce them.

One problem with the 1977 Protocols (specifically Protocol 2, which dealt with noninternational armed conflicts) was that they did not take seriously enough that restraint in warfare requires that the parties to a conflict be accountable if they flout such restraints. States can, in principle, be held accountable in ways that insurgent groups cannot. Groups that operate even more in the shadows, like terrorist groups, are even harder to hold accountable. Even the accountability of states is importantly dependent on self-policing. States have their own legal systems, which may explicitly or implicitly establish their own restraints on what members of their armed forces may do in wartime. Further, the pressure of public opinion exercises its own kind of constraint. Finally, though most fundamentally, states provide a focus for recognition and assertion of common values. Although this can backfire, as when a state uses such values to demonize its enemies, this can also be a profound source of moral backbone against such demonization and the flouting of restraint in war. Of course, not all states are equally good in these respects; thus, it is important that the effort to maintain restraint in war also imply an effort to create and support states that have robust legal systems, incorporating respect for human rights with provision for free exercise and expression of opinion among their populations, and that nurture and protect respect for moral value. Restraint in war ultimately depends on the self-policing of states having such character, and the 1977 Protocols did not recognize this.

States may, in fact, be the most important agents for the protection of the provisions for restraint in war. The behavior of states in regard to the established provisions and, more broadly, in regard to the moral ideas on which they are based—including respect for human rights as a universal value and commitment to protecting innocence while punishing guilt—sends a powerful message to nonstate groups engaged in armed conflict. States that have used terrorist methods or supported nonstate terrorist groups are an important part of the problem with terrorism. States that engage in internal oppression of elements of their population for reasons like difference in race, ethnicity, language, and religion and that use harsh treatment against them, including such methods as forcible resettlement, wholesale detention, arbitrary execution, and torture, give the message to nonstate groups that either oppose them or identify with them that such methods are all right. There are, of course, too many states that engage in such practices routinely. But the behavior of other states, like the United States, which seek to uphold democratic self-government, freedom, human rights, and respect for law, and in which respect for fundamental moral values is deeply embedded, is important as a positive model, but is perhaps even more so as a negative model, when such states engage in behavior that violates or even comes close to violating the established legal and moral restraints.

Lastly, those committed to the religious and moral traditions in which the provisions for restraint in armed conflict are rooted have their own special responsibility for the protection of those provisions. In the present historical context, I am thinking in particular of the responsibility of normative mainstream Muslims to oppose the radical version of Islam employed to justify a jihad against not only the United States but the West and Western culture in general. When this opposition comes from outside, it looks like a clash of civilizations—in this case, the radicals accuse the West of waging a new crusade against Muslims and against Islam everywhere. Given the nature of the threat posed by radical jihadism, such opposition from outside is necessary to defend Western societies and the values borne within Western culture. When Western scholars point out that the radical jihadists misinterpret Islam to their own purposes, the radicals and their fellow travelers can discount this as part of the crusade against Islam as a whole. But when Muslims within the normative mainstream make the same point, and when it is made strongly and universally enough that it cannot be denied, then the radicals cannot any longer claim Islam as the justification for their engaging in terrorism. Such ostracizing of individuals and groups who target noncombatants and seek indiscriminate and disproportionate weapons may ultimately be the best way to cope with them; it is certainly an important part of the entire answer.

I do not think, though, that anybody at this point knows what will finally be required to end the violations of noncombatant rights and the threat that WMD may be used against a noncombatant population. I only affirm that it is necessary to seek a solution and to keep on trying to do so.

## TAKING THE AIM OF PEACE SERIOUSLY

What does it mean that a justified war should aim at peace? What should be the characteristics of such peace? What responsibilities does this aim entail?

As I write this, elections have been held in Afghanistan, preparations are under way for elections and a new national government in Iraq, and the Palestinians under Mahmoud Abbas, the elected successor to Yasser Arafat, seem to be moving toward a rejection of terror and a possibility of some sort of settlement of the conflict with Israel. Bosnia has become relatively stable, and Kosovo, although still plagued by many problems, has moved significantly towards the goal of an orderly, just, and peaceful society. One might continue by listing the other conflicts that have raged in the last decade or more and have been brought, by either internal or external efforts or some mixture of the two, to some form of peace.

Peace, understood in the moral terms of the just war tradition, is not simply the absence of armed conflict. Indeed, to have a peaceful society implies that there will still, as needed, be some use of force against the enemies of that peace, the justice that feeds peace, and the order that embodies peace. The peace at which a just war should aim is not the absolute peace of the city of God, or its analog in other religions, either: it is the "tranquillity of order," as Augustine put it. Such a peaceful order, though, requires justice, a concept that includes such fundamental values as freedom, respect for human rights, protection of minorities from the tyranny of the majority, and provision for basic security in regard to fundamental human needs. That justice must be embodied in order means that these values must be institutionalized socially and legally; there must be rule of law, which must be undergirded by social dispositions and attitudes that support such law. To speak of peace only in terms of order would not only imply the possibility that this order might be unjust but it would suggest that peace is something static. Rather, since peace comes from an order that embodies and expresses justice, and since the demands for maintaining justice continually change, the peace at which good politics aims is a dynamic reality, ever responding to new challenges against it.

Such is the peace of a well-ordered, well-run society. The question is, though, how much of this is the responsibility of those who employ armed force when they aim at restoring or establishing peace in areas that have fallen victim to disorder, injustice, or both. For armed force cannot by itself establish peace; yet, it is a necessary component when threats to peace continue to run high. That means that one may not simply declare armed conflict to be at an end and then withdraw all armed forces, for that would create a vacuum, which the forces of injustice can quickly fill up. It is not necessary for such forces to remain until all the elements of a just, enduring, peaceful order have been established, but there is a responsibility to keep in place an armed presence sufficient to maintain order at least until the society in question is clearly on its way toward the peace that is aimed for.

As I have argued in other contexts when speaking about military intervention to stop and correct egregious violations of human rights, the cases of Bosnia and Kosovo offer many lessons for what is needed to establish peace. This includes a peacekeeping or stabilization force to create the necessary conditions for order and deal with the forces of injustice. The order such a force creates should also embody justice, expressed minimally in evenhanded treatment of competing claims, establishment and maintenance of a legal structure in accord with recognized standards for justice, and an effort to work with the citizens of the society in question, not bullying them or treating them as subjects, so that they can begin to take responsibility for structuring their own personal and communal lives. But the cases of Bosnia and Kosovo also teach us that more than the presence of an ordering military force is needed: it is necessary to assist the society in question in every way in which its essential institutions and ability to function have been destroyed or corrupted. Establishing the conditions for peace may thus include rebuilding the economy—not just providing economic aid but restoring the economic functioning of the society to health. It will likely include rebuilding the legal system, possibly from a state of deep corruption or a very low level of functionality. In Kosovo, for example, there was no functioning legal system at all: no law code, no police, no courts, only a small number of legally trained people and no schools to train them, and so on. The entire system had to be rebuilt virtually from scratch, and doing so required a long-term commitment of different kinds of people and resources. Both Bosnia and Kosovo also teach that the establishment of a society meeting even minimal standards for order, justice, and peace is likely to take years, not weeks or months, and may take generations of effort by people both within and outside of the society. Finally, these two cases also teach us the value of having international involvement as broad as possible in the effort to rebuild and reestablish a peaceful society.

Because the war to oust Saddam Hussein and his regime was justified as an effort to create a new order in Iraq—a society no longer ruled by the forces of tyranny and reestablished on the basis of democracy, freedom, and all the other aspects of genuine justice—it was a war that expressed the intention of creating peace. Having this intention is an important first step, but to aim at peace does not mean only having an intention; it means taking the responsibility to achieve that peace at least up to the level I have described. There were important failures in actuality, and these worked against peace rather than for it. The forces that succeeded so quickly in toppling the armed forces of the old regime were insufficient to establish and maintain postwar order; thus, rather than maintaining order, they were reduced to punishing disorder. Insufficient attention was given to the problems of establishing democratic social and political life in a society that had for more than a generation been ruled by a pervasive, invasive tyranny. Disagreement as to who would be in charge of the reconstruction efforts confused them at the beginning, during a critical time. And although there has been an international component to the rebuilding effort, the United States, for various reasons, has been the dominant presence across the board, in military as well as civilian aspects. But on the positive side, the United States has accepted the responsibility for establishing at least a minimally democratic order in Iraq and for providing a continuing presence so long as it is needed. At this writing, it remains unclear how well the effort to establish peace will succeed, for that depends finally on the Iraqis themselves, but there is a good chance that it will. In the end, being willing to shoulder the responsibility to carry through on the aim of peace after a conflict does not guarantee the establishment of peace. There are many other factors, different for every society, and many others have their own responsibilities, which may or may not be met. As in responsible parenting or responsible citizenship, responsibility lies in doing one's best and continuing to do it as long as it is helpful. Thus, I think the United States has shown its commitment to the end of peace in Iraq after Saddam Hussein, and I would apply this same standard to possible uses of armed force in the future.

## WHAT ABOUT THE CLASH OF CIVILIZATIONS?

We end where we began: Is there a clash of civilizations between America and the West, on the one hand, and the religion and culture of Islam on the other? Osama bin Laden, Ayman al-Zawahiri, and their associates, who later became known as the leaders of al Qaeda, said that such a clash exists in the 1998 declaration discussed in chapter 1. Putting it this way provides its own answer: certainly from the point of view of that declaration, these two civilizations are at war, and it is a war to the death. But that statement was intentionally the rationale for the campaign of terrorism that began soon after. It was not intended to provide a balanced judgment on relations between these civilizations but to issue a call to arms. The radical Islamism espoused by al Qaeda misuses normative Islamic tradition, although it purports to represent that tradition, and only a fraction of Muslims follow this radical form of Islam, although al Qaeda purports to speak for all Muslims. From the point of view of radical Islamism, Islam and the West are locked in a conflict that can only end when one of the combatants—the radicals think it will be the West—is vanquished and its civilization snuffed out. But the radicals are also locked in combat with the normative religious tradition of Islam and with the broad scope of Islamic history, as well as with the majority of contemporary Muslims, who do not hold to their brand of Islam. So, there is not one clash of civilizations here, but two. America and the West are involved in a clash not with the civilization of Islam as a whole but with the radical misappropriation of it used as a justifying ideology for implacable hatred and terrorism against the West. But the enemy of America and the West is also the enemy of Islam, and it needs to be combated from within as well as from without.

From the standpoint of al Qaeda and the radical Islamism it expresses, Muslims living in Western societies represent a potential fifth column to be used to undermine those societies. But from the perspective of the fight against radicalism and terror, the possibilities already actualized by many of those same Muslims and their children for personal freedom, for participation in democratic government, for cooperation with others in societies that respect and protect a plurality of religions and national and cultural backgrounds, and for prosperity and happiness in their lives represent a powerful argument against the view of the world put forward by the radicals. Indeed, so far as these people have had a positive experience of life in Western societies, they may constitute the most powerful refutation of radical Islamism and the radical clash-of-civilizations argument.

A critical issue is the relation of religion to society. For the radical Islamists, right religion is tied inseparably to the existence of a good society. Indeed, the dar al-islam of classical Islamic thought is at once a religious and political entity, governed by a leader in the succession of the prophet Muhammad (who was at once a religious and political leader) and ruled according to Muslim law. Although philosophers like the medieval thinker Abu Nasr Muhammad al-Farabi sought to define a political theory in which government could be legitimate even though the ruler was not also the supreme religious authority, the juristic conception of the religiopolitical dar al-islam as the ideal society remained pervasive; it is this that the radicals draw on today, and because of its heritage and long persistence, it is hard to refute. The best refutation is not theoretical but empirical: historically and contemporarily, states and empires in the sphere of Islamic civilization have separated the religious and secular functions in government. That such government, not least in recent history, has sometimes been bad government helps to feed the resurgent ideal of a religiopolitical order founded on a fundamentalist conception of Islam. But the historical experience has not always or inevitably been bad, and it is not universally bad today. In particular, it is not bad for Muslims who choose to participate in the political life of Western societies.

Still, there is a deep-rooted intellectual problem that has to be dealt with: how should religion be related to secular government? Does the separation of the two mean that the secular must be triumphant, with religion relegated not just to the sphere of private life but to social and political irrelevance? Versions of this view are well known in the contemporary Middle East, for such is the general approach shared by communist doctrine (and Soviet practice), by Turkey after Kemal Ataturk, and by French political and intellectual life. What is much less known and even less understood is how religion and the political order are related in American society, where even though there is a formal separation between institutional religion and the sphere of government, that separation is not absolute, and religion is treated positively not only or mainly in the private lives of individuals but importantly in the social or communal sphere. Secularism simply does not mean the same thing in this context as it does in the other ones mentioned. There is a role for religion in the public sphere, and religion is respected there for what it can contribute to the common life of the nation. Nor does the religion in question have to be a single one: the U.S. Constitution's provision that there not be an established national religion opened the door for religious pluralism, whose forms have continued to increase. Islam has found a place (rather, it is finding one since the process is dynamic rather than static), and the idea of a clash of civilizations based on religious difference alone within American culture—in effect, religious persecution—is deeply contradictory to this deep stream in American public life. One way of defusing cross-civilizational mistrust, where it exists, and undercutting a conception that is central to radical Islam's war against America and the West is to make this model, and the history that embodies it, more widely known. Muslims who have experienced it by participating in it may have a particular importance in doing this.

Finally, returning explicitly to just war tradition, this is not a tradition of holy war. Rather, as it first came together in the Middle Ages, it developed around conceptions that rejected holy war. Sovereign authority was defined as the highest temporal authority in a given political community. Just cause was defined in terms of response to threats to the common good of that community or actual damage to that common good. Right intention was defined, negatively, as the avoidance of motivations that were evil in the sense of what they would do in this life, not in terms of sins against the divine order; at the same time, it was defined positively as the aim of establishing or restoring a peaceful, thus just, social order. The concept of just war thus assumed secular government from the first, even though it clearly drew on values and conceptions defined and transmitted religiously. The idea of jihad of the sword is something different: as classically stated, it requires authorization by the supreme leader, who is at once supreme in both religious and political authority; and its fundamental justification is to protect the rule of Islamic law and to extend it throughout the world. As stated by contemporary radical Islamists, the religious justification remains, although the authority to wage such war rests with each individual Muslim. But jihad in Islamic religion is not simply a form of using armed force; it is a term that refers more basically to the striving, in faith and action, to live out the religious faith to which Muslims are committed. There is a place for this in the tradition of religious pluralism, although there is no place here for a jihad of the sword that seeks to destroy that pluralism and the society and culture that have made it possible.

There is indeed a clash of civilizations with those who accept the conception of Islam set out by al Qaeda. They have made it so. But those who are in a war against this conception include not only America and the West but also Muslims opposed to it as a right understanding of the religion and culture of Islam. Between these last two, there is no such clash, and care must be taken to ensure that one does not develop.

# BIBLIOGRAPHY

Abedi, Mehdi, and Gary Legenhausen. *Jihad and Shahadat: Struggle and Martyrdom in Islam*. Houston, TX: Institute for Research and Islamic Studies, 1986.

Ajami, Fouad. "The Summoning." *Foreign Affairs*, vol. 72, no. 4 (September/October 1993), 2–9.

Augustine, Saint. *Letter to Boniface, no. clxxxix*. In *Fathers of the Church*. Washington, DC: Catholic University of America Press, 1951–56, vol. 4.

Carter, Jimmy. "Just War—Or a Just War?" *New York Times*, March 7, 2003, Section 4, 13.

Casey, Shaun, et al. "Statement of 100 Christian Ethicists." http://www.maxspeak .org/gm/archives/chron.htm (21 Dec. 2004).

Childress, James F. "Just War Theories: The Bases, Interrelations, Priorities, and Functions of Their Criteria." *Theological Studies*, vol. 39 (September 1978), 427–45.

Fussell, Paul. *The Great War and Modern Memory*. London: Oxford University Press, 1975.

Gregory, Bishop Wilton T. "Letter to President Bush," September 13, 2002. http:// www.usccb.org/sdwp/international/bush902.htm

Grotius, Hugo. *De Jure ac Pacis Libri Tres*. Translation of the edition of 1646 by Francis W. Kelsey, et al. *Classics of International Law*. Oxford: Clarendon Press; London: Humphrey Milford, 1925.

Huntington, Samuel P. "The Clash of Civilizations?" *Foreign Affairs*, vol. 72, no. 3 (Summer 1993), 22–49.

Institute for American Values. "What We're Fighting For: A Letter from America." February 2002. Http://www.americanvalues.org/html/wwff.html

———. "Pre-emption, Iraq, and Just War: A Statement of Principles." November 14, 2002. Http://www.americanvalues.org/html/1b___pre-emption.html

Jansen, Johannes J.G. *The Neglected Duty: The Creed of Sadat's Assassins and Islamic Resurgence in the Middle East*. New York: Macmillan, 1986.

Johnson, James Turner. *Just War Tradition and the Restraint of War*. Princeton: Princeton University Press, 1981.

———. *The Holy War Idea in Western and Islamic Traditions*. University Park, PA: The Pennsylvania State University Press, 1997.

———. *Morality and Contemporary Warfare*. New Haven: Yale University Press, 1999.

Johnson, James Turner, and George Weigel. *Just War and the Gulf War*. Washington, DC: Ethics and Public Policy Center, 1991.

Johnston, Douglas, and Cynthia Sampson, eds. *Religion: The Missing Dimension in Statecraft*. Oxford: Oxford University Press, 1994.

Keller, Bill. "Fear on the Home Front." *New York Times*, February 22, 2003, Section A, 17.

bin Laden, Osama, et al. "World Islamic Front Statement Urging Jihad against Jews and Crusaders." http://www.library.cornell.edu/colldev/mideast/wif.htm (Sept. 29, 2001).

Land, Richard D., et al. "Land's Letter to Bush on 'Just War,'" October 3, 2002. http://www.christianity.com/partner/Article_Display_Page

Miller, Judith. *God Has Ninety-Nine Names*. New York: Simon & Schuster, 1996.

National Conference of Catholic Bishops. *The Challenge of Peace*. Washington, DC: United States Catholic Conference, 1983.

———. *The Harvest of Justice Is Sown in Peace*. Washington, DC: United States Catholic Conference, 1993.

*New York Times*, March 19–April 15, 2003.

Peters, Rudolph. *Islam and Colonialism: The Doctrine of Jihad in Modern History*. The Hague: Mouton, 1979.

Ramsey, Paul. *War and the Christian Conscience: How Shall Modern War Be Conducted Justly?* Durham, N.C.: Duke University Press, 1961.

———. *The Just War: Force and Political Responsibility*. New York: Charles Scribner's Sons, 1968.

Roberts, Adam, and Richard Guelff, eds. *Documents on the Law of War*, 2d ed. Oxford: Clarendon Press, 1989.

Shriver, Donald W., Jr. "An Ethic of Humanitarian Intervention." In J.I. Coffey and Charles T. Mathewes, eds., *Religion, Law, and the Role of Force*. Ardsley, NY: Transnational Publishers, 2002.

Sullivan, Andrew. "This Is a Religious War." *New York Times Magazine*, October 7, 2001, 44.

United Methodist Bishops. *In Defense of Creation*. Nashville, TN: Graded Press, 1986.

United States Conference of Catholic Bishops. "Statement on Iraq," November 13, 2002. http://www.ctbi.org.uk/intaff/iraq/uscath01.htm

Walzer, Michael. *Just and Unjust Wars*. New York: Basic Books, 1977.

————. "What a Little War in Iraq Could Do." *New York Times,* March 9, 2003, Section A, 27.

Weeks, Albert L. "Do Civilizations Hold?" *Foreign Affairs,* vol. 72, no. 4 (September/October, 1993), 24–25.

Wright, Quincy. *A Study of War.* 2 vols. Chicago: University of Chicago Press, 1942.

# INDEX

Abbas, Mahmoud, 140
accidents of war, 94, 99
Afghanistan, 20, 64, 140
after the war, 113–46; conduct of war, 131–40; humanitarian intervention, 122–26; peace establishment, 140–43; preemptive use of force standards, 114–22; world order, 126–31
Ajami, Fouad, 4
all-or-nothing war. *See* total war
Amin, Idi, 63
Aquinas, Thomas, 25, 42, 66
Arabian Peninsula, 15
Arkin, William, 80
assassination of foreign leaders, 72, 74
asymmetrical warfare, 92–93
Ataturk, Kemal, 144
Augustine, Saint, 9, 18, 22, 24, 29, 66, 116, 129–30
authority: Catholic understanding of, 28–29, 30; for jihad of the sword, 11, 15–16; just war tradition and, 17, 18, 28–29, 37, 52; political responsibility and, 29, 37, 52, 67; pre-war debate and, 48, 60
al-Azhar, Shaykh, 13

bacteriological warfare, 99–100
*baraka* (blessing), 11, 12

before the war, 45–67; administration arguments for war, 45–47; humanitarian intervention, 56–57; international law, 54–56; just war principles, 53–54, 57–61; neglected just war principles, 62–67; preemptive use of force, 47–53
Bin Laden, Osama: on jihad, 12–16; on targets of terrorism, 18–19
Biological Weapons Convention (1972), 100
bombing, 34, 76, 79, 98–102. *See also* precision-guided munitions (PGMs)
Bosnia, 34, 56, 64, 109, 123–25, 133, 140–42
Britain, 34
bullets, exploding and expanding, 99–100
Bush, George H. W., 47
Bush, George W.: administration arguments for war, 45–47, 53–54; response of, to September 11 attacks, 5–6

caliph, 8
Cambodia, 63
car bombing, 87–88
Carter, Jimmy, 59–61, 76

Casey, Shaun, 50
Catholic Church: on just war, 17, 21; on sovereignty, 62; U.S. bishops on humanitarian intervention, 57, 122–23; U.S. bishops on just war, 26–32, 47–50, 57, 58, 66, 76, 116, 120
*The Challenge of Peace* (U.S. Catholic bishops), 26–29, 48, 58, 76
Cheney, Richard, 45
Childress, James F., 28
Christianity: and humanitarian intervention, 124; love and war in, 24–25; preemptive use of force opposition and, 47, 50; and self-defense, 116. *See also* Augustine, Saint; Catholic Church; Presbyterian Church; Protestantism; Southern Baptist Convention; United Methodist Church
circular error probable (CEP), 78–79
cities, moral issues in siege of, 106–7
city of God, 9, 129–30
civilians, 41, 81
Civil War, American, 89–90, 99–100, 105–6
clash of civilizations, 3–7, 14, 85, 140, 143–46
clear and present danger, 51
collateral damage, 20, 25, 34, 78, 80, 94
colonialism, 11–12, 117
conduct of war: accountability and, 138–39; Bin Laden and, 16; discrimination of targets, 19, 20–21, 24–26, 40–41, 76–77, 105; future, 131–40; irregular warfare, 89–93; Islamic, 83, 138–40; noncombatant immunity, 18–19, 26, 34, 39–41, 54, 80–83, 131–40; proportionality of harm, 17, 19, 20–21, 24–26, 40–41, 60, 76–77, 80, 99–102, 105; reciprocity principle and, 136–37; siege warfare and, 105–7; violating norms of, 34–35, 86–89, 94–98, 102–5, 131–33, 136;

weapons limitations, 19–20, 40, 77–80, 99–101, 105. *See also* international law of armed conflict; *jus in bello*
Congo, 133
consequentialist criteria, 17, 29, 34, 36–37, 49
Covenant of the League of Nations, 114
customary law, 92, 117, 120–21, 126–27, 136

*dar al-harb* (territory of war), 8–9, 82, 129
*dar al-islam* (territory of Islam), 8–9, 14, 82, 129–30, 144
dead, treatment of, 87
debates over war. *See* after the war; before the war; during the war
decapitation, military strategy of, 71–75
Declaration of Independence, 62
Declaration of the Rights of Man, 62
De Gaulle, Charles, 117
demonization of enemy, 137–38
deontological criteria, 17, 36
discrimination: intended versus unintended harm, 24–26; misapplying principle of, 40–41; modern warfare and, 40, 76–77; as secondary criterion, 19; siege warfare and, 105; weapons development and, 134–36; weapon type and, 20–21
disease. *See* bacteriological warfare
double effect. *See* rule of double effect
Douglass, James, 39
dual-use targets, 101–2
during the war, 71–109; decapitation, 71–75; irregular warfare, 89–93; jihad, 82–86; just war definition, 102–3; moral distinctions in harm, 93–94, 98–102; noncombatants, 80–82, 86–89, 93–94; peace establishment, 107–9; precision-guided muni-

tions, 75–80; siege warfare, 105–7; suicide bombing, 104–5; violating rules of war, 86–89, 94–98

Egypt, 52, 117
emir, 11
Enlightenment, 5, 130
European Union, 131
exploding and expanding bullets, 99–100

al-Farabi, Abu Nasr Muhammad, 144
fatwa, 13
fedayeen, 35, 86–87, 133, 137
*fiqh* (Islamic jurisprudence), 13–14
fog of war, 93
force, moral character of, 36, 48. *See also* use of force
France, 144
Franco-Prussian War, 106
Frederick the Great, 95
freedom. *See* personal liberty
Friedman, Tom, 55, 56, 63
Friesen, Duane, 50
fundamentalism: Islamic, 13–15, 84–86, 129, 139–40, 143–45; terrorism and, 6–7, 15; varieties of, 6–7
*fuqaha* (scholars), 13
Fussell, Paul, 95

gas warfare, 99
General Assembly of the Presbyterian Church, 123
Geneva Convention (1864), 87
Geneva Conventions (1949), 40, 81, 90
Geneva Protocol (1925), 100
Germany, 34
*ghazi* (leader in war), 11
Gratian, 66
Gregory, Wilton, 32, 47–50, 66
Grotius, Hugo, 52, 116
guerrilla warfare, 89

Gulf War (1990–1991), 4, 29, 47, 49, 55–56, 101, 128

Hague Convention IV (1907), 90
Hague Declaration 3 (1899), 100
Hamas, 84–85
Hauerwas, Stanley, 50
Hehir, Bryan, 21
holy war, 145. *See also* jihad of the sword
humanitarian intervention, 33–34, 56–57, 122–26
humanity, concept of, 105
human rights: Hussein's violations of, 34, 46, 56–57, 124–25; noncombatant immunity and, 138
human shields, 86–88
Huntington, Samuel P., 3–4, 7
Hussein, Qusay, 72
Hussein, Saddam: actions of, used to justify war, 46, 53; human rights violations by, 34, 46, 56–57, 124–25; rules of war violated by, 96; sovereignty argument used by, 62–63; targeting of, 71–75
Hussein, Uday, 72

imam, 8
Institute for American Values, 55
international cooperation, 64
international law: of armed conflict (*see* international law of armed conflict); enforcement of, as justification for war, 46, 54–56; European versus American/British understanding of, 126–27; on preemptive use of force, 114–15, 117, 121; on self-defense, 115, 117
international law of armed conflict: on conduct of war, 91–92, 100, 102–3; just war tradition and, 16, 33; on noncombatants, 19; preemptive use of

force and, 52–53; on weapons limitations, 40, 78. *See also* conduct of war
international order, 122, 126–31
Iran, 52
Iraq: reconstruction of, 64–66, 108–9, 140, 142–43; as victim of U.S. aggression, 15–16. *See also* after the war; before the war; during the war; Gulf War (1990–1991); Operation Iraqi Freedom
irregular warfare, 89–93
Islam: basis of, 8; on conduct of war, 83, 138–40; mainstream versus radical, 13–14, 139–40, 143–44; and non-Islamic world, 8–16, 82–86, 129–30; radical, 13–15, 84–86, 129, 139–40, 143–45; religion and politics in, 5–6, 8, 144–45; rulers in, 8, 10; terrorism and, 6; on use of force, 7
Israel, 12, 52, 84, 117–18
Ivory Coast, 133

jihad of the sword: authority for, 11, 15–16; Bin Laden on, 12–16; of collective duty (*see* jihad of the sword: offensive versus defensive); of individual duty (*see* jihad of the sword: offensive versus defensive); offensive versus defensive, 9–16, 82–86; tradition of, 7, 8–12, 145; world order and, 130
John Paul II, 123
Jomini, Henri de, 106
*jus ad bellum*, 17–19; *jus in bello* substituted for, 25–26, 37, 39, 102–3
*jus in bello*, 17, 19–22; substituted for *jus ad bellum*, 25–26, 37, 39, 102–3. *See also* conduct of war
just cause, 18, 28–29, 48, 54, 56
justice: Catholic bishops on, 30; just war to protect, 17, 18, 22, 36, 141
just war: Bush (George H. W.) and, 47; contemporary application of principles, 38; controversies over, 23–42; holy war versus, 145; humanitarian intervention and, 124–25; neglected issues in, 62–67; Operation Iraqi Freedom debate and, 47–51, 57–61; preemptive use of force and, 116–17, 121; primary versus secondary criteria for, 17, 29, 36–37, 57; prudential criteria for, 17, 29, 36–37, 49, 57; Ramsey on, 23–26; tradition of, 7, 16–22, 33, 35–42, 145; U.S. bishops on, 26–32, 47–50, 57, 58, 66; values underlying, 35–36; Walzer on, 32–35; world order and, 129–30

Keller, Bill, 55, 56
Kellogg, Frank, 115
Kosovo, 34, 56, 64, 109, 123–25, 140–42

Land, Richard D., 53–54, 65
last resort, 29, 54, 57–60, 116
liberty. *See* personal liberty
Lieber, Francis, 89–90, 99–100
limits of war. *See* conduct of war
love, 24–25
Luther, Martin, 42

Maimonides, 106
means of war, limitations on, 19–21, 40, 77–80, 83, 91–93, 99–101, 105, 131–40
Meyers, Richard E., 102
military: conduct-of-war training for, 134; just war concept in, 17, 33, 81
militias. *See* irregular warfare
Miller, Judith, 6
Milošević, Slobodan, 57, 62
modernity, 15
modern warfare: discrimination and proportionality of, 76–77, 80; pacifism arising from, 26, 49

Monroe Doctrine, 117
moralists, 20, 24, 29, 37, 52, 67, 100, 135
Muhammad, 8

National Council of Churches, 21
National Defense Strategy (NDS), 119
national interests, 123–25
National Security Strategy (NSS) 2003, 119
nation-states: accountability of, for conduct of war, 138–39; political role of, 3–5; religion's role in, 5; sovereignty of, 126–28; terrorism used or sponsored by, 139
*New York Times*, 6, 58
1967 Middle East war, 52, 117–18
noncombatants: categories of, 39–40, 80–81, 87; eroding protection of, 86–89, 94–98, 104–5; harm to, moral distinctions in, 24–26, 93–94, 98–102; human rights of, 138; immunity of, 18–19, 26, 34, 39–41, 54, 80–83, 131–40; land and property of, 106; obligations to, 26, 34, 80–82, 86–89; sentiments of, 41; siege warfare and, 105–7
Noriega, Manuel, 63
North Korea, 52
nuclear weapons, 24, 26, 28, 49, 78–79, 117

Omar, Mullah, 10
Operation Desert Storm. *See* Gulf War (1990–1991)
Operation Iraqi Freedom: air campaign in, 34; Catholic bishops on war with, 31–32; conduct of war in, 35, 131–34; proportionality principle in, 41. *See also* after the war; before the war; during the war
order: humanitarian intervention to preserve international, 122; just war to protect, 18, 22, 36, 129, 140–41; world, 126–31
overwhelming force, 77, 131–33

pacifism, 50; Catholic Church and, 28, 32; just war reasoning and, 39; modern-war, 26, 49
Pact of Paris (Kellogg-Briand Pact, 1928), 114–15, 117
Palestinians, 12, 140
Panama, 63
paramilitary. *See* irregular warfare
partisan warfare, 89
PBS (Public Broadcasting Service), 75
peace: as aim of just war, 17, 18, 22, 29, 30–31, 36, 48, 63–64, 67, 140–41; establishment of, 64–67, 108–9, 141–43
personal liberty, 64–65
PGMs. *See* precision-guided munitions
political realism, 3–5
Pol Pot, 63
Powell, Colin, 51
power grid destruction, 101
precision-guided munitions (PGMs), 20–21, 75–76, 78–80
preemptive use of force: Bush administration arguments for, 45–46; Catholic bishops on, 31–32; critiques of, 47–51; focus on, as misguided, 51–53, 119; against Iraq, 45–51, 118–20; 1967 Middle East war and, 52, 117–18; standards for, 52–53, 114–22
Presbyterian Church, 57, 123
presumption against war, 26–28, 29, 32, 35–36, 47–51, 76
prisoners, treatment of, 87
probability of success, 29, 54
proportionality: double-effect reasoning and, 101–2; future harm and, 60; in-

nocents and, 24–26; misapplying principle of, 40–41, 132; modern warfare and, 76–77; PGMs and, 20–21, 80; rules of war in conflict with, 99–101; as secondary criterion, 17, 19, 29; siege warfare and, 105; weapon type and, 20–21, 76–77, 80
Protestantism, on sovereignty, 62
Protocols to Geneva Conventions (1977), 40, 41, 81, 90, 138–39

al Qaeda: jihad according to, 12–16, 84–85, 143; religious basis of, 5–6; and WMD, 114

Ramsey, Paul, 19, 23–26, 39, 40, 49, 67, 99–100, 116, 122, 134
Rantisi, Abdel Aziz, 82
Reagan, Ronald, 28, 118
reciprocity principle, conduct of war and, 136–37
regime change, 31–32, 63–64
religion: jihad and authority of, 13–14; pluralism of, 145; political influence of, 4–6, 8, 144–45; terrorism and, 6. See also Christianity; fundamentalism; Islam
right intention, 17, 18, 31, 54, 73–74
Ross, W. D., 28
rule of double effect, 20, 25, 34, 78, 101, 105
rulers, in Islam, 8, 10, 14
rules of war. See conduct of war; international law of armed conflict
Rumsfeld, Donald, 45
Rwanda, 34, 56, 123–25, 133

Sadat, Anwar, 14
Saladin, 11, 12
Saudi Arabia, 15, 85
self-defense, 115–17
self-sacrifice, 104

sharia (Islamic law), 14, 15
Shiite tradition, 8, 10
siege warfare, 105–7
Sierra Leone, 133
Somalia, 34, 123
Southern Baptist Convention, 53
sovereignty: moral versus political sense of, 62–63, 125; UN and state, 126–28
Spain, 89
Stassen, Glen, 50
states. See nation-states
success. See probability of success
suicide bombing, 85, 104–5
Sullivan, Andrew, 6
Sunni tradition, 8, 10
supreme emergency, 34–35
surrender, feigning, 86–89
Syria, 52, 117

Tanzania, 63
terrorism: Islamic fundamentalism and, 15; moral response to, 16–22; religion and, 6–7; states and, 139; supreme emergency concept and, 34–35; targets of, 19; and violation of norms of conduct, 34–35
total war, 92, 97, 103
truces, honoring of, 55–56
Turkey, 144

Uganda, 63
unilateralism, 66
United Methodist Church, 21
United Nations: authority of, 61; on preemptive use of force, 115, 127; Protocol on Non-Detectable Fragments (1980), 100; Security Council, 55; shortcomings of, 128; and state sovereignty, 126–28; suicide bombing of, 85; world order and, 126–27
United States: conduct of Iraqi war by,

133–34; international responsibility of, 122, 131; religion and politics in, 144–45; represented as aggressors, 15–16
Universal Declaration of Human Rights (1948), 138
U.S. Conference of Catholic Bishops, 32, 48–49
use of force: aggressor-defender model, 53; overwhelming force, 77, 131–33; West versus Islam on, 7. *See also* jihad of the sword; just war
U.S. Presbyterian Church, 57
utilitarianism. *See* consequentialist criteria

victory, definition of, 107–9
Vietnam, 63
Vietnam War, 49, 99
virtue, 81, 88–89, 97
Vitoria, Francisco de, 42, 66

Walzer, Michael, 32–33, 58–59, 106, 116, 122

war, causes of, 3–4. *See also* conduct of war; jihad of the sword; just war
war crimes tribunals, 63
warfare. *See* conduct of war; irregular warfare; modern warfare; siege warfare
weapons: development of discriminating, 134–36; limitations on, 19–20, 40, 77–80, 99–101, 105; nuclear, 24, 26, 28, 49, 78–79, 117; PGMs, 19–21, 75–76, 78–80
weapons of mass destruction (WMD), 45, 52–53, 114, 119–20
Weeks, Albert L., 4
West, versus Islam on use of force, 7
Westphalian system, 52–53, 62–63, 117
world order, 122, 126–31
World War I, 96
World War II, 34, 106
worst-case scenarios, 37, 49–50, 60
Wright, Quincy, 3–4, 7

Yugoslavia, 106

Zaire, 133
al-Zawahiri, Ayman, 13

# ABOUT THE AUTHOR

**James Turner Johnson** (Ph.D., Princeton, 1968) is a professor of religion and an associate member of the graduate program in political science at Rutgers, The State University of New Jersey, where he has been on the faculty since 1969.

Johnson has received Rockefeller, Guggenheim, and National Endowment for the Humanities fellowships and various other research grants and has directed two NEH summer seminars for college teachers. His books include *Ideology, Reason, and the Limitation of War*, *Just War Tradition and the Restraint of War*, *Can Modern War Be Just?*, *The Quest for Peace: Three Moral Traditions in Western Cultural History*, *The Holy War Idea in Western and Islamic Traditions*, *Moral Issues in Contemporary War*, and (edited with John Kelsay) *Cross, Crescent, and Sword: The Justification and Limitation of War in Western and Islamic Tradition* and *Just War and Jihad: Historical and Theoretical Perspectives on War and Peace in Western and Islamic Traditions*. Johnson is coeditor of the *Journal of Military Ethics*; a trustee, editorial board member, and former general editor of *The Journal of Religious Ethics*; and a member of professional societies in the fields of religion and political science. He has lectured to academic, military, and general audiences in the United States and abroad. He is married (since 1969) to Pamela B. Johnson; they have two grown children.